The Casual Vineyard Table

The Casual Vineyard Table

FROM WENTE VINEYARDS

CAROLYN WENTE • KIMBALL JONES

Photography by Richard Eskite

TEN SPEED PRESS

Berkeley/Toronto

A Kirsty Melville Book

Ten Speed Press
PO Box 7123
Berkeley, California 94707
www.tenspeed.com

Distributed in Australia by Simon and Schuster Australia, in Canada by Ten
Speed Press Canada, in New Zealand by Southern Publishers Group, in South
Africa by Real Books, and in the United Kingdom and Europe by Airlift Book
Company.

Cover and text design by Carol Salvin
Food styling by Kimball Jones
Prop styling by Carol Hacker

Library of Congress Cataloging-in-Publication Data
Wente, Carolyn.
The casual vineyard table : from Wente Vineyards / Carolyn Wente and
Kimball Jones.
    p. cm.
Includes index.
ISBN 1-58008-485-0
1. Cookery. 2. Wine and wine making. I. Jones, Kimball. II. Wente Vineyards
Restaurant. III. Title.

TX714 .W3596   2003
641.5'09794'65–dc21   2002154599

First printing, 2003
Printed in China

1 2 3 4 5 6 7 8 9 10 — 07 06 05 04 03

Contents

Acknowledgments

From both of us . . .

First and foremost, thank you to Carol Salvin, our coordinator, designer, word-smither, scheduler, and co-conspirator. We value all her support, guidance, nudging, and creativity in our projects, especially *The Casual Vineyard Table*. To everyone at Ten Speed Press, in particular Kirsty Melville, our publisher, and Holly Taines White, our editor, for their belief in our food and wine and for publishing our recipes. A hearty thank you to Eskite Photography: Richard, Juliann, and Melissa. Their patience, experience, and can-do energy show in all the photography in this book.

This recipe collection would not be what it is without the efforts of our recipe testers—our everyday cooks who analyze how the recipes work and provide feedback on taste and presentation. Thank you to Alison Bagley, Virginia Cook, Liz Greist, Andrew Groth, Judy Groth, Shirley Jones, Josie Little, Moaya Scheiman, Marilyn Schlangen, Nancy Schultz, John Watanabe, and Jennifer Whitmer.

From Carolyn . . .

To my husband, Buck, and our son, Bucky, who are always eager to try what Mom cooks up, with plenty of encouragement and feedback. I also want to express my appreciation to the great team we have at Wente Vineyards; you all work extremely hard to make great wine and superb food that we are able to share with everyone who comes to visit us in the Livermore Valley. And, always a special thanks to friends and family who support our experimentation and exploration of food and wine on a daily basis.

From Kimball . . .

To my wife, Suzanne, who makes cooking fun for me and brightens every day. To my sons, Morgwn and Taylor; my parents, Richard and Shirley; and everyone in my family for trying all of the recipes, even the ones that didn't work! Thank you to the Groths for providing inspiration, encouragement, and great wine. Thanks Moaya, my partner in crime, emergency recipe tester, and oldest friend. Thank you to everyone at Wente Vineyards Restaurant for their commitment to excellence, most notably Michelle Lyon, Scott Ritchie, and Elisabeth Schwarz.

Thoughts from Carolyn and Kimball

To us, the casual vineyard table is surrounded by everyday ease. A sense of well-being and balance emanates from its planning and preparation, the flavors of its food and wine, and the company of family and friends. If you approach the table feeling the strains of a busy life, it will provide a place to gather together, reflect, and be replenished with nourishment and companionship. It will infuse you with a renewed sense of energy, purpose, and balance.

The food we prepare for this table transforms simple concepts into balanced, complex flavors. And, it is almost always served with wine. Because of our lifelong involvement with wine, both as a livelihood and as a lifestyle, and our belief that wine is one of the fundamental ingredients in meal preparation, our recipes are wine-friendly creations. We usually have a particular style of wine in mind (and probably a bottle open!) when we are working in the kitchen.

The straightforward techniques we use treat our ingredients respectfully, magnifying and enhancing their natural flavors. For example, in some recipes we roast or caramelize vegetables and meats to deepen their flavors; we use marinades and vinaigrettes to add flavor and complexity; and employ simple sauces such as pestos, aiolis, and salsas to add freshness and sparkle. Nothing is masked or overpowered. Because our simple approach requires fewer ingredients, it demands the use of the best possible fixings available. The obvious choices are fresh, local, seasonal offerings. At their peak, they are the most flavorful, plentiful, and the easiest on the pocketbook.

Balancing flavor is a cornerstone for us when we are working with food and wine. A harmony among the sweet, savory, salty, and acidic characteristics inherent in a dish will give it a delicious, full, round complexity. With these tastes working in concert, this enjoyable dish will be a perfect partner for any wine. If one or more flavors are too dominant or out of proportion, it will affect the perceived taste of the wine. Sweet and savory, by themselves or as predominant flavors, will make a wine taste stronger and more alcoholic, with its fruity notes and/or sweetness considerably diminished. Saltiness and acidity will make a wine taste milder, less alcoholic, less bitter and astringent, with increased fruit flavors. Most people will be somewhat forgiving if a dish's stronger saltiness and acidity make a wine seem milder. However, few people enjoy a wine that is overpowering because of the sweetness in the accompanying dish. It's helpful to remember this: when preparing a meal, if a dish seems too sweet, add a squeeze of lemon juice or a pinch of salt; if the dish is too acidic, try a little sugar to balance it. Adjusting the flavors in a recipe or selecting a wine with a particular flavor profile can have an effect on all the flavors in a meal. A perfect pairing is a flavor-balanced dish that will let a wine taste true to its style and character. And, most importantly, tastes good to you!

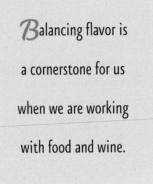

Balancing flavor is a cornerstone for us when we are working with food and wine.

Though we have suggested some of our favorite varietals as pairings, enjoy the balanced recipes in this cookbook with any wine that you like. In most cases, we have listed several options because we all have individual palates and more than just one wine pairs well with each recipe. The best match of a dish with a particular wine is a personal preference.

This balanced approach to creating dishes and meals was our guiding principle as we developed the recipes for this book. We culled our own personal notes, experiences, and recipes, looking for distinctive flavors, simple ingredients, and ease of preparation. The recipes presented here are those we serve to our families and friends at our casual vineyard tables. Most of them can be cooked quite easily for a weekday evening meal. Since a casual meal embraces variety and informality, we have organized these recipes into Small Bites, Big Bites, and Desserts—offering an invitation to mix and match. A selection of two or three small bites could comprise a Sunday brunch, an afternoon get-together, or a family dinner. A big bite and a simple salad could make an easy after-work meal.

So, the casual vineyard table finds us, gathered together, with food and wine in balance, nourishing ourselves, and bringing harmony to our lives. Such repasts allow us to slow down and catch up with each other. If you are brought to the table, reflect on the wine and food you are enjoying. Cooking is an experiment; these recipes are proven experiments. Try something new. It is an exquisite exploration of the senses that can be shared with friends and family.

A Simple Taste Test

Take a piece of sweet fruit, such as mango; a wedge of lemon; and some salt. (No, it is not some new Martini!) Open a bottle of your favorite wine and pour yourself a glass. (This will work with any wine.) Take a sip of wine, then a bite of fruit. Taste the wine again. For most people, the wine will taste stronger, with a considerable lack of the fruit flavors. Now taste a little squeeze of lemon juice and try the wine again. In general, most people perceive the wine as milder and fruitier. Now squeeze a little lemon juice and a pinch of salt on another slice of mango. Taste this combination and then taste the wine. The salt and acidity help to balance the sweetness of the mango, which helps to pair it better with the wine, making the wine taste truer to its actual style and flavor.

Small Bites

These recipes can be served when you just want a little something,
or they can be combined with other dishes to create fuller fare.
Browse through these if you are looking for . . .

Something different for breakfast

A soup and a salad

A lighter dinner

First and second courses for a dinner party

A side dish to accompany an entrée

Finger food for entertaining

Brunch ideas

A quick, elegant, late-night bite

Two or three dishes to serve for dinner

Cantaloupe and Shrimp Salad

⅓ cup freshly squeezed lime juice
   (about 4 limes)

2 tablespoons rice wine vinegar

1 large cantaloupe, cut into
   ½-inch dice (about 4 cups)

½ teaspoon kosher salt

½ teaspoon freshly ground
   black pepper

1 tablespoon minced peeled
   fresh ginger

¼ cup minced red onion

¼ cup coarsely chopped fresh basil

¼ cup coarsely chopped fresh mint

1 pound medium (31 to 35 count)
   shrimp, peeled, deveined,
   and cooked

½ cup pecans, toasted and chopped
   (page 118)

1 cup seedless red Flame grapes, halved

2 ripe avocados, pitted and halved

Juice and finely grated zest of 1 lemon

2 to 3 tablespoons aioli (page 110)

Try this recipe chilled on a warm summer day. In fact, by refrigerating before serving, the flavors marry, making the salad's sweet-sour contrast even better. This particular medley of tastes (the cantaloupe-vinegar-lime juice and the mint-ginger-basil) comes together in a dish that a number of wines will enhance. Crisp white wines and dry Rosés are among my favorites to serve with it. GW

In a small bowl, stir together the lime juice and vinegar. In a large bowl, combine the cantaloupe, salt, pepper, ginger, onion, basil, and mint. Toss gently. Add the shrimp, pecans, grapes, and lime juice mixture and toss again. Taste and adjust the seasonings if necessary. Cover and refrigerate for at least 20 minutes or up to 2 hours.

To serve, peel an avocado half and cut lengthwise into ¼-inch slices. Fan the slices on a plate. Repeat with the remaining avocado halves. Squeeze lemon juice over the avocados to prevent them from browning, and garnish with lemon zest. Using a slotted spoon, divide the melon and shrimp among the 4 plates, placing a scoop at the base of each avocado fan. Garnish with aioli and serve immediately.

Black-Eyed Pea Chopped Salad with Spicy Italian Sausage

Serves 6

I like the bit of heat that the spicy sausage adds to this chopped salad, but you can substitute any of your favorites. There are so many available—chicken with sun-dried tomatoes, chicken with artichoke, Polish sausages, or the milder Italian varieties. This recipe can be made without the sausage too, as a lighter side dish or vegetarian alternative. You could also cook the sausage on the stovetop in a grill pan. With the myriad of vegetables and the bit of spice in this salad, try dry white wines with good acidity, such as Sauvignon Blanc, Pinot Grigio, or Pinot Blanc. GW

4 (6-inch) fat spicy Italian sausages

1½ cups dried black-eyed peas

1 teaspoon kosher salt

3 cups water

Freshly ground black pepper

⅓ cup pistachios, toasted and skinned (page 118)

1 cucumber, peeled, seeded, and diced

½ small red onion, diced

3 green onions, including white and green parts, chopped

3 red tomatoes, seeded and diced

2 yellow tomatoes, seeded and diced

⅓ cup chopped cilantro

2 tablespoons freshly squeezed lemon juice

Prepare a medium fire in a charcoal grill or preheat a gas grill to medium. Place the sausages on the grill rack and grill, turning frequently, for about 10 minutes, until browned and cooked through. Remove from the grill and allow to cool.

While the sausages are grilling, combine the black-eyed peas, salt, and water in a saucepan over high heat. Cover and bring to a boil. Decrease the heat to low and cook for 15 minutes, or until tender but still a little crunchy. Drain and place in a large bowl. Season with salt and pepper while the peas are warm so the seasonings are absorbed. Add the pistachios, cucumber, red and green onions, tomatoes, and cilantro and mix well. Cut the sausages into ½-inch slices and add to the peas. Toss gently. Add the lemon juice and salt and pepper to taste and toss again.

Serve immediately while still warm, or refrigerate until ready to eat.

Jicama-Mango Salad with Ginger-Lime Vinaigrette

Serves 4

1 teaspoon finely minced lime zest

1 tablespoon freshly squeezed
   lime juice

1 teaspoon finely minced shallot

2 teaspoons finely minced or
   shredded peeled fresh ginger

3 tablespoons extra virgin olive oil

3 cups julienned jicama
   (about a 1-pound jicama)

1 large mango, peeled and julienned

Kosher salt and freshly ground
   black pepper

This is an incredibly refreshing salad, great for spring or summer, and a wonderful accompaniment to simply prepared seafood such as steamed crab, lobster, or shrimp. If you like a little heat, you can add ¹/₄ teaspoon of cayenne pepper to the dressing. You can also substitute other fleshy, sweet fruits such as peaches, nectarines, or papaya for the mango. The lime helps to offset the sugars of the mango. However, because it is difficult to completely balance that sweetness, I like this salad with a wine that also has a little sweetness, such as an off-dry Riesling, Gewürztraminer, or a sweeter-style Champagne or sparkling wine such as Extra-Dry or Demi-Sec. KJ

In a large bowl, combine the lime zest, lime juice, shallot, and ginger. Whisk in the olive oil. Add the jicama and mango and toss well. Season with salt and pepper and toss again. Divide among 4 plates and serve immediately.

Couscous Salad with Tomatoes, Cucumber, Opal Basil, and Olives

Serves 4

The balance of textures and flavors in this salad makes it a wonderful foil for roasted or grilled meats, fish, or fowl—a great candidate for a summer party or a picnic. I especially like using opal basil, a member of the mint family used primarily in Thai cooking. Its richly aromatic flavors and slight mint overtones add a tantalizing note, but you could certainly use other types of basil. You can also spice up the couscous by adding minced chile peppers or ground cayenne pepper. Bring a dry Rosé or a Sauvignon Blanc along to share with this salad. KJ

In a saucepan over high heat, bring the water and olive oil to a boil. Stir in the couscous and return to a boil. Decrease the heat to achieve a simmer, cover, and cook for 5 minutes. Remove from the heat and let stand, covered, for 10 to 15 minutes, until the water is absorbed and the grains are tender. Fluff with a fork to separate the grains, and spread on a baking sheet. Season with salt and pepper and cool in the refrigerator for at least 15 minutes.

Cut the cucumber on the diagonal into ¼-inch slices. In a bowl, combine the cucumber, tomato, basil, olives, vinegar, and couscous and toss well. Add salt and pepper to taste. Adjust the seasoning with additional basil and vinegar if necessary. Serve cold or at room temperature.

2¼ cups water

1 tablespoon plus 1½ teaspoons extra virgin olive oil

1½ cups couscous

Kosher salt and freshly ground black pepper

1 English cucumber, peeled, halved lengthwise, and seeded

1 vine-ripened tomato (preferably an heirloom such as Brandywine or Marvel Stripe), cored, seeded, and cut into ¼-inch dice

2 tablespoons finely sliced fresh opal basil, more as needed

¼ cup pitted small green olives (such as Picholine)

2 teaspoons sherry vinegar, more as needed

Butter Lettuce Salad with Fuyu Persimmons and Camembert Toasts

2 heads butter lettuce

1 tablespoon apple cider or juice

2 tablespoons apple cider vinegar

½ teaspoon honey

1 teaspoon Dijon mustard

½ cup extra virgin olive oil

Kosher salt and freshly ground
   black pepper

4 thin slices baguette, cut on the
   diagonal to 4 inches long

1 (4-ounce) round ripe Camembert

1 Fuyu persimmon, cut into
   ¼-inch slices

This recipe only works with Fuyu persimmons because they have none of the astringency of Hachiya persimmons, the other variety commonly found in the United States. Hachiyas are too tannic to eat without cooking—the astringency causes your mouth to dry out. Fuyus, however, can be eaten out of hand, as you would an apple. Fuyu persimmons resemble tomatoes in shape, with a bright orange and red skin, and are best when they are hard. If you can't find Fuyus, try using pears or apples. The soft, creamy Camembert on crisp baguette toast adds a nice textural balance to the dish. I like a light fruity wine such as Riesling, Gewürztraminer, or Pinot Blanc with this salad. KJ

Preheat the broiler.

Clean the lettuce and separate the leaves, tearing the larger leaves into bite-sized pieces. To make a vinaigrette, whisk together the cider, vinegar, honey, and mustard in a large bowl. Slowly whisk in the olive oil and season with salt and pepper.

Cut each slice of baguette in half lengthwise. Spread on a baking sheet and toast under the broiler until golden brown. Remove the toast from the broiler and spread with the Camembert. Toss the lettuce and persimmon slices in the vinaigrette. Divide the salad among 4 plates, arranging the persimmon on top of the lettuce. Serve with 2 pieces of the cheese toast on each plate.

Minted Watermelon and Multicolored Tomato Salad

1 (4-pound) seedless watermelon

2 pounds vine-ripened orange or yellow tomatoes (about 8)

1 teaspoon kosher salt

½ red onion, cut into ⅛-inch slices, rings separated (about ⅓ cup)

1 lemon cucumber or ½ small regular cucumber, thinly sliced into rounds

2 tablespoons freshly squeezed lime juice

1 teaspoon grated peeled fresh ginger

1 teaspoon sugar

2 tablespoons julienned fresh mint, for garnish

When I prepare this dish, I don't chill the salad since the ingredients lose flavor when cold. During one of the photo sessions for this book, we had a bowlful in the shade of a large tree. As the session was wrapping up, the tasting began. This salad was quickly devoured, a refreshing end to a long day.

To provide a wonderful visual contrast to the watermelon, use yellow or orange varieties of tomatoes. Of course, you can always use red tomatoes if the other colors can't be found. If you are not a fan of mint, substitute cilantro or flat-leaf parsley. Try this fruit salad with a slightly chilled, dry Rosé-style wine. There are many "pink" wines that are crisp with full fruit flavors, without residual sugar. These wines are often overlooked, but their flavor profiles and acidity can be a pleasant surprise when combined with light summer salads such as this. GW

Remove the rind and any seeds from the watermelon and cut into bite-sized pieces over a colander set over a large bowl. Put the pieces into the colander once cut, trying to catch as much of the juice as you can. You should have about 8 cups of watermelon pieces. Cut each tomato into 6 wedges and add to the watermelon in the colander. Sprinkle the fruit with the salt and toss well. Let stand for 45 minutes at room temperature to allow the juices to drain into the bowl.

Remove the colander from the bowl and pour the fruit juices into a saucepan. Place over medium heat and simmer until reduced to about 3 tablespoons, 5 to 10 minutes. Transfer the fruit to the bowl, add the onion and cucumber, and toss well.

In a small bowl, combine the reduced juices, lime juice, ginger, and sugar. Pour over the watermelon mixture and toss gently to coat well. Garnish with the mint and serve immediately.

Chilled Zucchini Soup with White Truffle Oil

All gardeners are familiar with the bountiful zucchini plant. It is one of the earlier producers, quickly taking over the garden and soon providing squash for the entire neighborhood. This soup uses garden-fresh zucchini to make a wonderfully rich, thick soup. Serve it with a medium-bodied Chardonnay or a well-chilled, dry Rosé and thick slices of crusty country bread dipped in olive oil. A cool approach to a summer lunch. GW

Place the zucchini and salt in a saucepan with just enough water to barely cover. Bring to a boil over high heat. Decrease the heat and simmer, uncovered, for 2 minutes, or until tender. Remove from the heat, drain, and place in a bowl.

Heat a sauté pan over medium-high heat and add the butter. When the butter is melted, add the onion and tarragon and sauté for about 4 minutes, until the onion is translucent. Remove from the heat and add to the zucchini. In batches if necessary, transfer the vegetables to a blender or food processor and purée with the cream cheese and wine. Return the purée to the bowl and stir in enough stock to make a thick, creamy, smooth consistency. Cover and place in the refrigerator until chilled, about 30 minutes. Taste and adjust the seasoning with salt and pepper if necessary.

To serve, divide the soup among 4 bowls. Drizzle white truffle oil in the center of each serving. Garnish with chopped parsley and lemon zest and serve immediately.

6 zucchini (about 3 pounds), cut into ¾-inch slices

½ teaspoon kosher salt

1 tablespoon unsalted butter

1 yellow onion, chopped

1 teaspoon chopped fresh tarragon

8 ounces cream cheese, cut into 1-inch chunks

1 cup Chardonnay or dry white wine

About 4 cups cold chicken stock (page 111)

Freshly ground black pepper

Garnish

2 teaspoons white truffle oil

1 tablespoon finely chopped fresh flat-leaf parsley

1 teaspoon finely grated lemon zest

Chilled Asparagus Soup with Smoked Salmon and Lemon-Chive Oil

1 tablespoon olive oil

1½ cups sliced leek, white part only

2 bunches asparagus (about 30 spears), trimmed, peeled, and coarsely chopped

1 russet potato, peeled and cut into ¼-inch dice

3 cups chicken stock (page 111)

Kosher salt and freshly ground white pepper

2 teaspoons freshly squeezed lemon juice

1 tablespoon finely chopped lemon zest

1 tablespoon finely sliced chives

3 tablespoons extra virgin olive oil

4 asparagus spears, thinly sliced diagonally, for garnish

¼ pound cold-smoked salmon, cut into thin strips, for garnish

Asparagus is notoriously difficult to pair with wine. There is something in its skin that makes many wines taste grassy, herbaceous, and medicinal. By peeling the asparagus, you eliminate this tendency. Instead of trimming the asparagus ends with a knife, I snap them off: hold the ends of a stalk and bend until it snaps. It will usually break where the stalk begins to toughen and turn white, leaving you with the tenderest part to eat. The crisp flavors of fresh asparagus and lemon are a zingy accompaniment to Sauvignon Blanc or just about any dry, crisp white wine. The salmon adds a contrasting smokiness to the clean essence of this spring soup. *KJ*

Heat a nonreactive saucepan over medium-high heat and add the oil. When the oil is hot, add the leek and half of the chopped asparagus. Decrease the heat to medium-low, cover, and cook, stirring occasionally, until the vegetables begin to release some of their liquid, about 10 minutes. Add the potato and stock and bring to a simmer, covered, for 10 minutes, or until the potatoes are very tender. In batches, transfer to a blender, add the remaining chopped asparagus, and purée until very smooth. Transfer to a bowl and season with salt, pepper, and lemon juice. Cool over an ice bath if you want to serve it right away. Otherwise, cover and refrigerate until chilled, stirring occasionally.

In a small bowl, combine the lemon zest, chives, and extra virgin olive oil and mix well.

To serve, divide the soup among 4 bowls. Garnish with the sliced asparagus and the smoked salmon. Drizzle the lemon-chive oil onto the soup and serve immediately.

Sharp Cheddar Chowder with Pepper Twists

Each Christmas I receive a wheel of Cheddar cheese from a friend. By mid-January, I am usually looking for ways to use my gift. One of my winter favorites, potato and leek soup, seemed a perfect place to start. The sharpness of the cheese nicely contrasts with the sweet, creamy potatoes and leeks. The pepper in the pastry twists also adds a little edge. The twists can be made up to three days ahead of time if you store them in an airtight container or a reseal-able freezer bag. If you need a shortcut, you can make the twists with store-bought frozen puff pastry. Either way, they are a nice accompaniment to this rich soup. A full-bodied Chardonnay will pair well; the fruitiness of an off-dry Riesling or a Viognier would also make a good match. GW

¼ recipe pastry sticks dough (page 113)

1 teaspoon freshly ground black pepper

¼ teaspoon ground cayenne pepper

6 tablespoons unsalted butter

2 cloves garlic, finely chopped

2 yellow onions, chopped

1 leek, white part only, finely sliced

2 cups peeled and chopped carrots (about 6 carrots)

1 large potato, peeled and cut into ¼-inch dice

½ teaspoon ground mustard

4 cups chicken stock (page 111)

1 cup Riesling

2 cups grated sharp Cheddar cheese

Dash of Tabasco sauce

Kosher salt

2 tablespoons finely chopped fresh chives, for garnish

To make the twists, follow the basic pastry sticks recipe, rolling the dough into a ⅛-inch-thick rectangle and brushing with egg wash. In a small bowl, combine the black pepper and cayenne. Sprinkle the mixture evenly over the dough. Roll the dough once more, pressing the pepper mixture into the dough. Cut the dough as described in the basic recipe. As each stick is transferred to the baking sheet, twist it a couple of times lengthwise. Bake per the basic recipe instructions.

To make the soup, heat a soup pot over medium heat and add the butter. When it is melted, add the garlic, onions, and leek and sauté for 3 to 5 minutes, until translucent but not colored. Decrease the heat to low and add the carrots and potato. Cook, stirring occasionally, until tender, about 20 minutes. Increase the heat to high, add the mustard, stock, and wine, and bring to a boil. Decrease the heat to low and simmer for about 25 minutes, until the flavors are integrated and the vegetables are tender. Remove from the heat and let stand for about 10 minutes.

Pass the soup through a medium-meshed sieve, reserving the liquid. In batches, transfer the solids to a blender or food processor and purée. You may need to add some of the liquid to help in the puréeing. Return the purée to the pot over medium heat. Stir in enough of the reserved liquid for the soup to be moderately hearty and thick in texture. Add the cheese and Tabasco and stir until the cheese melts. Add more of the reserved stock if the soup is too thick. Season with salt and pepper.

To serve, ladle the soup into 6 bowls and garnish with chives. Pass a basket filled with the pepper twists.

Heirloom Tomato Soup with Poached Pacific Salmon and Basil Oil

Serves 4

This is a wonderful, refreshing cold soup to serve with Sauvignon Blanc, Chardonnay, or even a slightly chilled Pinot Noir. Finding excellent-quality tomatoes is the key to this great summer treat. KJ

Reserve 1 tomato. Core the remaining tomatoes, cut into chunks, and place in a blender (you may have to do this in several batches). Purée until smooth. Pass through a medium-meshed sieve or a China cap strainer into a bowl. Season to taste with salt and balsamic vinegar. Cover and refrigerate.

Season the salmon with salt and pepper on both sides. Quarter the reserved tomato. To make a liquid for poaching the salmon, combine the tomato, onion, shallot, celery, garlic, peppercorns, bay leaves, wine, corn cob, and water in a nonreactive pot over high heat. Bring to a boil, then decrease the heat, and cook at a medium simmer for 30 minutes. Pass through a medium-meshed sieve and return the liquid to the pot. Discard the solids.

Bring the liquid back to a simmer over medium heat and add the salmon. Decrease the heat to achieve a very low simmer and poach the salmon until still a little pink inside, about 10 minutes, depending on the thickness of the salmon. Remove from the liquid, place in a bowl, and allow to cool. Discard the poaching liquid. Flake the salmon with a fork. Add the corn kernels, bell peppers, and chile. Season to taste with salt and pepper and toss gently.

Combine the basil and olive oil in a mini chopper and process until puréed. Season with salt and pepper to taste.

To serve, remove the soup from the refrigerator and ladle into bowls. Garnish the center of each serving with the salmon mixture and drizzle with the basil oil. Serve immediately.

---

5 pounds heirloom tomatoes, such as Brandywine, Marvel Stripe, or a vine-ripened variety

Kosher salt

Balsamic vinegar

½ pound skinless Pacific salmon fillet (can substitute Atlantic or farm-raised salmon)

Freshly ground black pepper

½ cup sliced yellow onion

1 shallot, sliced

1 celery stalk, sliced

2 cloves garlic

½ teaspoon black peppercorns

4 bay leaves

1½ cups white wine, such as Sauvignon Blanc or Chardonnay

Kernels from 1 ear corn, cob saved for the poaching liquid

4 cups water

1 tablespoon diced red bell pepper

1 tablespoon diced yellow bell pepper

1 teaspoon diced poblano chile

½ cup firmly packed fresh basil leaves

½ cup extra virgin olive oil

Lentil-Apple Soup

1 tablespoon olive oil

1 large leek, white part only, thinly
   sliced (about 1 cup)

1 apple, peeled, cored, and diced
   (about 1 cup)

1 cup white wine, preferably
   Sauvignon Blanc

1 cup apple juice or cider

About 2 cups chicken stock
   (page 111)

1 cup lentils

2 bay leaves

1½ cups peeled and diced Yukon gold
   or any white potatoes, reserved in
   water (about ½ pound)

Kosher salt and freshly ground
   black pepper

Juice of 1 lemon

1 teaspoon minced fresh thyme

2 teaspoons minced fresh
   flat-leaf parsley

¼ cup toasted bread crumbs
   (page 110)

Among all of the dried beans and peas, lentils are one of my favorites. They are easy to use since they do not need to be soaked in water before cooking. Lentils also have an earthiness that I like using in vegetable stocks to round out the flavors of other ingredients. I've used Fuji and Gravenstein apples in this soup, but you can use any apple with a nice balance of sweetness and tartness. I think Granny Smiths are too tart. We have served this soup at home with everything from a crisp Sauvignon Blanc to an earthy Zinfandel, so pick your favorite and enjoy! KJ

Heat a nonreactive saucepan over medium-high heat and add the olive oil. When the oil is hot, add the leek and apple and cook, stirring often, for 10 minutes, until light golden brown. Add the wine and apple juice and scrape the toasted bits from the bottom of the pan. Add the stock, lentils, and bay leaves. Bring to a boil, decrease the heat to achieve a simmer, and cook for about 30 minutes, until the lentils are just starting to get tender.

Drain the potatoes, add to the pan, and return to a simmer. Simmer for about 15 minutes, until the potatoes are tender. Remove from the heat and season with salt and pepper. Remove the bay leaves and discard. In batches if necessary, transfer the soup to a food processor or blender and purée until smooth. Return to the pan and taste and adjust the seasoning with salt, pepper, and lemon juice if necessary. You may also need to add a little more stock if the soup is too thick.

In a small bowl, combine the thyme, parsley, and bread crumbs. Ladle the soup into 4 large bowls. Garnish with the seasoned bread crumbs and serve immediately.

English Peas, Sugar Snap Peas, Snow Peas, and Pearl Onions

The variety of peas in this recipe creates an interesting texture and a pleasing visual presentation. Peas can be slightly sweet, so when partnering this dish with a dry red or white wine, you may want to squeeze some lemon juice over the mixture before serving to balance the flavors. GW

Place the onions in a saucepan with water to cover and bring to a boil over high heat. Remove from the heat, drain, place in cold water, and drain again. Remove the outer skin by gently trimming off the root end, then squeezing the other end of the onion between your index finger and thumb—the onion should squirt out of the skin in one piece.

In a large sauté pan, combine all of the peas with 1 cup salted water. Cover and bring to a boil. Steam for about 5 minutes, or until the peas are a brilliant shade of green but still crunchy. Do not overcook. Remove from the heat and drain.

Return the peas to the sauté pan and place over medium-high heat. Add the onions, butter, and rosemary. Sauté for 2 minutes, stirring to coat the peas and onions. Season with salt and pepper and serve immediately.

1 cup white and red pearl onions

1 cup shelled fresh English peas

1 cup fresh sugar snap peas, strings removed

1 cup fresh snow peas, strings removed

2 tablespoons unsalted butter

1½ tablespoons finely chopped fresh rosemary

Kosher salt and freshly ground black pepper

Grilled Herb-Marinated Artichokes

4 large artichokes

¼ cup balsamic vinegar

½ cup olive oil

Juice of 2 lemons (about ¼ cup)

¼ cup mixed chopped fresh herbs such as rosemary, tarragon, oregano, chervil, and marjoram

Select large artichokes for this recipe because they will be easier to handle when quartered. You may find it difficult to fit all of the artichokes into one pot, so I sometimes use two or more. The artichokes can be made a day or two in advance and served cold, with aioli or homemade mayonnaise as a dip. Artichokes contain a bitter component called cynarin, which makes wine—and everything else you taste—seem sweeter. The balsamic vinegar and lemon juice in this dish help to balance that sweetening effect. Dry, crisp wines, which are more acidic, are therefore enhanced. Try the artichokes with Sauvignon Blanc or a crisp, non–barrel fermented Chardonnay.   GW

With a pair of scissors, clip off the tip of each artichoke leaf. Trim the stems and place the artichokes in a pot large enough to allow each choke to sit on the bottom. Fill the pot with enough salted water to cover the artichokes halfway. Cover the pot and bring to a boil. Decrease the heat and simmer for about 30 minutes, until a small knife inserted into the bottom of an artichoke feels little resistance. Immediately remove the artichokes from the water and place in a strainer.

In a small bowl, whisk together the vinegar, olive oil, lemon juice, and the herbs.

When the artichokes are cool enough to handle, cut them into quarters. A serrated knife works best to cut through the tougher, outer leaves. With a fork, gently remove the center choke and discard. Place the artichokes in a large resealable plastic bag, pour the marinade over them, seal the bag, and toss gently. If you prefer, you can use a nonreactive bowl for marinating the artichokes. Marinate, turning occasionally, at room temperature or in the refrigerator for 2 to 3 hours.

Prepare a medium-hot fire in a charcoal grill or preheat a gas grill to medium-high. Place the artichokes on the grill rack and grill, turning once, for 5 to 6 minutes on each side, enough to warm through and add a smoky flavor. Serve hot.

French Fillet Beans with Caramelized Shallots, Bacon, and Hazelnuts

Serves 4

Green beans are at their absolute peak during the summer and fall. Any small, young green bean can be used if you can't find fillet beans, but you may have to adjust your cooking time. If you use larger green beans, you can always slice them lengthwise. I originally prepared this for a Thanksgiving feast, but it could accompany most meats and poultry. If you want to make this dish without the bacon, substitute 1 tablespoon of olive oil for the bacon fat. The wine that you serve with the main course should be a fine accompaniment. KJ

1 pound French fillet or Blue Lake green beans, stem ends trimmed

2 thick bacon strips, diced

4 shallots, quartered lengthwise

¼ cup toasted, peeled, and chopped hazelnuts (page 118)

Kosher salt and freshly ground black pepper

Bring a large pot of salted water to a boil over high heat. Add the beans and cook until just tender, 3 to 4 minutes. Drain in a colander.

Heat a sauté pan over medium heat. Add the bacon and cook until most of the fat is rendered and the bacon becomes a little crispy, about 10 minutes. With a slotted spoon, remove the bacon from the pan and transfer to paper towels to drain. Add the shallots to the bacon fat, still over medium heat. Cook, stirring frequently, until caramelized and golden brown, about 5 minutes. Drain off most of the fat, leaving about 2 tablespoons. Add the blanched beans and cook until lightly browned, about 5 minutes. Add the bacon and hazelnuts, season with salt and pepper to taste, and mix well. Serve immediately.

Charred Radicchio

Radicchio, a chicory, is part of the daisy family, which includes escarole, endive, Belgian endive, and frisée. The bitterness in all chicories calls for a preparation emphasizing a little sweetness and acidity to balance the bitterness. I love this radicchio with roasted chicken or beef tri-tip and would serve it with the wine that complements the main dish. *KJ*

1 tablespoon balsamic vinegar

3 tablespoons olive oil

Kosher salt and freshly ground black pepper

1 large head radicchio

In a bowl, whisk together the balsamic vinegar and olive oil. Season with salt and pepper. Cut the radicchio into quarters through the stem. Remove any brown outer leaves. Toss the radicchio in the vinegar and oil. Let marinate for 10 minutes.

Heat a grill pan over high heat. Add the marinated radicchio and brown, turning once, for 3 to 4 minutes on each cut side, until lightly charred. Remove from the heat and serve immediately.

Serves 4

Sweet Potatoes with Lemon-Honey Butter

I find sweet potatoes at most Thanksgiving dinners to be too sweet, especially when marshmallows are added. In this recipe, the natural sugar of the sweet potatoes is balanced by the acidity of lemons and by lavender, a very aromatic and underused herb. Because the dish is still a little sweet, I prefer a slightly sweet or off-dry version of Riesling, Gewürztraminer, or Pinot Gris. *KJ*

2 tablespoons olive oil

4 sprigs lavender, tops only, coarsely chopped

Kosher salt and freshly ground black pepper

2 large sweet potatoes, unpeeled, ends trimmed, sliced into 1½-inch rounds

¼ cup unsalted butter, at room temperature

1 tablespoon lavender honey or any other honey

Finely grated zest of 2 lemons

Preheat the oven to 375°F.

In a bowl, combine the olive oil and lavender. Add salt and pepper to taste. Add the sweet potatoes and toss to coat evenly. Place the rounds on a baking sheet, a cut side down. Sprinkle with any remaining lavender mixture. Place in the oven and cook until the potatoes are browned nicely on one side, about 15 minutes. Turn the potatoes and brown the other side, another 15 minutes, or until easily pierced with a knife.

In a large bowl, combine the butter, honey, and lemon zest. Add the hot sweet potatoes, toss to coat, and serve immediately.

Maple-Herb Roasted Nuts

My first catering chef, Ron Goodell, and I collaborated on this recipe. It can be made with any combination of nuts, but I really like this particular mixture. Rosemary and lavender are usually growing in our garden, so they are almost always in the herb mix. We have a hard time keeping these nuts on the buffet tables during our concert series at the winery. KJ

Preheat the oven to 350°F.

In a large bowl, combine the pecans, almonds, walnuts, oil, maple syrup, herbs, and cayenne pepper. Toss to coat evenly. Spread on a baking sheet and roast for 15 minutes, or until golden brown and toasted. Stir and turn the nuts halfway through cooking so they toast evenly. The nuts will start sticking to each other and the pan when they are almost done. Remove from the oven and allow to cool, tossing frequently while cooling to prevent sticking. When the nuts are just cool enough to handle, sprinkle liberally with salt and pepper to taste and toss well.

Serve immediately, store in an airtight container at room temperature for up to 2 weeks, or freeze for up to 1 month. If frozen, refresh after thawing by spreading on a baking sheet and warming in a 350°F oven for 3 to 5 minutes.

2 cups whole shelled pecans (about 8 ounces)

2 cups whole shelled almonds (about 10 ounces)

2 cups whole shelled walnuts (about 8 ounces)

2 tablespoons olive oil

1/4 cup pure maple syrup

2 tablespoons mixed finely chopped fresh herbs such as rosemary, sage, marjoram, savory, thyme, lavender, and oregano

1/4 teaspoon ground cayenne pepper

Kosher salt and freshly ground black pepper

Dungeness Crab and Meyer Lemon Phyllo Triangles with Arugula Salad

¼ pound baby spinach

½ pound fresh Dungeness crabmeat, picked over for shell

1 Meyer lemon, sectioned and membranes removed

Zest of 2 Meyer lemons, finely chopped

½ cup crème fraîche (page 112)

3 (14 by 18-inch) sheets phyllo dough

Olive oil, for brushing

2 teaspoons white sesame seeds

2 teaspoons black sesame seeds

Juice of 1 Meyer lemon

½ teaspoon minced shallot

½ teaspoon Dijon mustard

1 teaspoon sherry vinegar

1 tablespoon extra virgin olive oil

2 cups loosely packed arugula

I developed this recipe for a dinner I did with Carolyn at the James Beard House in New York City. I wanted to combine the spinach and phyllo I had seen on menus during a recent trip to Turkey with two quintessentially California ingredients—Dungeness crab and Meyer lemon. I added the black and white sesame seeds to give the phyllo triangles a nice color balance, but if you can't find the black, you can just use white ones. We served a dry California Chardonnay that evening, but this recipe really lends itself to any crisp white wine. KJ

Bring a large pot of salted water to a boil. Fill a large bowl with ice water. Plunge the spinach into the boiling water until it turns bright green, about 30 seconds. Immediately remove from the boiling water with a slotted spoon and plunge into the ice water. Immediately remove from the ice water with a slotted spoon and place in a clean kitchen towel. Gently squeeze out as much water as you can. Transfer to a cutting board and chop coarsely. Place in a bowl and add the crab, lemon sections, half of the lemon zest, and 1 tablespoon of the crème fraîche. Stir gently to mix.

Preheat the oven to 375°F.

On a clean work surface, lay out 1 sheet of phyllo dough. Brush with olive oil and sprinkle lightly with one-third of the black and white sesame seeds. Repeat twice, adding 2 more layers of dough and seeds. Cut the dough in half lengthwise, then cut each half into rectangles about 3 inches wide and 7 inches long to get 12 pieces of dough total.

Place 1 tablespoon of the filling at one end of a piece of dough. Starting from the short end, fold the lower corner up over the filling to form a triangle. Keep folding in a triangle shape, until you have a tight triangle, tucking under the final edge. (See illustration on page 28.) Repeat with the remaining filling and dough pieces. Brush the triangles with more olive oil, place on a baking sheet, and bake until golden brown, 15 to 20 minutes.

(continued)

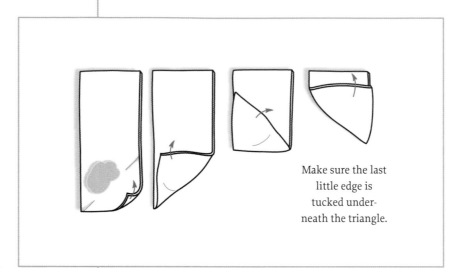

Make sure the last little edge is tucked underneath the triangle.

In a small bowl, combine the remaining lemon zest and crème fraîche and mix well. Add a squeeze of lemon juice to taste.

In a bowl, whisk together the shallot, mustard, and vinegar. Whisk in the olive oil. Add the arugula and toss well to coat.

To serve, place a small mound of arugula on each plate. Top with 2 to 3 phyllo triangles and drizzle with some of the zested crème fraîche. Serve immediately.

Sweet Pea Toasts with Spicy Coppa

This is an easy appetizer to make when you are in a hurry, especially if you can get your kids to shell the peas! Frozen peas will work, but these toasts are best with fresh ones. Blending the peas results in a delightfully creamy texture that is further enhanced by extra virgin olive oil. The sparkle of chervil, the fruitiness of olive oil, and the balancing tartness of lemon all add intriguing flavor highlights. If you can't find coppa, a spicy or mild cured sausage made from the shoulder of the pig, you could substitute salami. For a vegetarian appetizer, use a little shaved Parmesan cheese instead of coppa and add some chile flakes if you want a little heat. I like a crisp, dry Rosé, Sauvignon Blanc, or Chardonnay with this dish. KJ

2 cups shelled fresh sweet English peas (about 2¼ pounds fresh in the pod)

2 tablespoons extra virgin olive oil, more for drizzling

½ teaspoon finely minced lemon zest

2 teaspoons freshly squeezed lemon juice

1 teaspoon minced fresh chervil or thyme

Kosher salt and freshly ground black pepper

1 baguette

¼ pound spicy coppa, very finely julienned

Preheat the broiler.

Over high heat, bring a large saucepan of water and 2 tablespoons salt to a boil. Add the peas and cook until just tender, 3 to 4 minutes. Drain in a colander and transfer to a small food processor. Process until all of the peas are broken down but not smooth. You do not want to purée them—a little texture is just fine.

Transfer the peas to a bowl and add the olive oil, lemon zest, lemon juice, and chervil. Season with salt and pepper and mix well. Slice the baguette on a slight diagonal into ¼-inch pieces. Place the bread on a baking sheet and drizzle with olive oil. Toast under the broiler until light golden brown.

To serve, spread the pea purée on the toasts and top with a little mound of coppa. Serve immediately.

Potato-Parsnip Cakes with Smoked Sturgeon

Serves 4

½ cup peeled and grated parsnip

1½ cups finely julienned Yukon gold
   potatoes (2 to 3 potatoes)

4 teaspoons all-purpose flour

1 egg

Kosher salt and freshly ground
   black pepper

2 tablespoons olive oil, more as needed

¼ cup crème fraîche (page 112)
   or sour cream

1 teaspoon freshly squeezed
   lemon juice

1 green onion

¼ pound smoked sturgeon,
   thinly sliced

A perfect partner for Champagne! This is one of my favorite New Year's Eve and special-occasion recipes. You can serve the potato-parsnip cakes with any smoked fish or fowl or even caviar. The potatoes need to be finely julienned to make them the right texture for the cakes—I find that a mandoline works great for this. These cakes are similar to latkes, but use flour rather than matzo meal for binding. KJ

Preheat the oven to 350°F.

In a bowl, combine the parsnip, potatoes, flour, and egg. Season with salt and pepper. In ¼-cup amounts, form the mixture into 4 cakes about ½ inch thick and 2 inches wide.

Heat a large sauté pan over medium-high heat and add enough of the oil to coat the bottom of the pan. When the oil is hot, add the cakes without crowding (you may have to do this in batches). Cook until golden brown and crispy on the first side, 4 to 5 minutes. Turn the cakes over and cook until the second side is browned, 4 to 5 minutes. Place on a baking sheet as they are done. Add a little more oil after the first batch if needed. When all of the cakes have been browned, place in the oven and finish cooking for another 15 minutes, until cooked through.

In a small bowl, combine the crème fraîche and lemon juice. Slice the green part of the green onion very thinly on an extreme angle. To serve, place 1 cake on each plate. Top each with smoked sturgeon, crème fraîche, and green onion. Serve immediately.

Flatbread with Peaches, Farmer's Cheese, Prosciutto, and Arugula

Makes 4 flatbreads or 48 appetizers

Flatbreads are a great starting place for appetizers: only the season and your imagination limit their toppings. The success of this particular combination depends on the fruit being ripe and full of flavor. You can also make this palate-teaser with nectarines, figs, or mangoes. Just make sure the fruit has a firm yet ripe texture. If you want an assortment of flavors, prepare only half of this recipe's topping ingredients and create a different combination for the other two pieces of dough. Another one of my favorites is thinly sliced caramelized onion, diced Granny Smith apple, and crumbled blue cheese. If you don't have a pizza paddle and stone, assemble and bake the flatbread on baking sheets. A sparkling wine is always a good choice with starters. *KJ*

½ recipe pizza dough, divided into 4 pieces (page 114)

4 ounces fresh farmer's or mild goat cheese, crumbled

2 ripe peaches, thinly sliced and tossed with lemon juice

2 teaspoons freshly squeezed lemon juice

8 slices prosciutto

¼ pound baby arugula (about 50 leaves), or regular leaves cut into chiffonade

Prepare the oven for pizza baking as described on page 117; preheat it to 500°F. Dust a pizza paddle with flour.

Working with one piece of dough at a time, stretch it with flour-dusted hands into a round about ⅛ inch thick (or as thin as you can make it without tearing it) and about 8 inches in diameter. Place on the pizza paddle and sprinkle with one-fourth of the cheese. Arrange one-fourth of the peach slices on the cheese. Slide the flatbread from the paddle onto the pizza stone in the oven. Cook for about 6 minutes, until the edges and bottom are a rich golden brown. If any bubbles form in the dough, pierce with a sharp knife. Repeat with the remaining pieces of dough, cheese, and peaches. As you take each flatbread out of the oven, slide the next one in. Or, if your pizza stone is large enough, you can cook two or more at a time.

As you remove each flatbread from the oven, sprinkle with ½ teaspoon of the lemon juice, cover with 2 slices of prosciutto, and cut into 12 wedges. Top each wedge with an arugula leaf and serve immediately.

Corn Cakes with Pacific Salmon, Heirloom Tomatoes, and Basil

Serves 4

These corn cakes can be used much like blini and are wonderful served with smoked fish, braised duck, or even roasted chicken. You can add fresh corn, bell peppers, or green onions to the mix to impart extra flavor and texture. It's very important to get the heat exactly right for these silver dollar–sized cakes; if the heat is too hot, you'll burn them up. I don't oil the pan as there is butter in the batter. This recipe will make about 24 cakes, well more than what you need, but I always find that I lose a few getting the pan to the perfect temperature, so it's good to have some extra. This summer dish is equally enjoyable with Chardonnay, Rosé Champagne, or Pinot Noir. *KJ*

Preheat the oven to 200°F.

To prepare the corn cakes, in a bowl, mix together the cornmeal, salt, flour, and sugar. With your fingers, work the butter into the dry ingredients until there are no lumps larger than a grain of rice. In a small bowl, whisk together the buttermilk and egg. Add to the dry ingredients and combine quickly with a few strokes, just until incorporated. Do not overmix.

Warm a griddle or a cast-iron skillet over medium-high heat. Drop tablespoons of batter onto the hot surface to make silver dollar–sized cakes. Cook, turning once, for about 1 minute on each side, until golden brown. Turn down the heat if the cakes are coming out too dark. You should have at least 12 cakes, or 3 per person. Cover with a damp towel and keep warm in the oven until ready to assemble.

Season the salmon with salt and pepper. Heat a nonstick sauté pan over high heat and add the olive oil. When the oil is hot, add the salmon without crowding (you may have to cook in batches). Sear until golden brown on the underside, about 1 minute. Turn and cook the other side for 1 minute, until golden brown. Transfer to a plate.

In a small bowl, toss the tomatoes with the lemon juice and season with salt and pepper.

To assemble, place a corn cake on each plate. Add a small dollop of crème fraîche and top with a piece of salmon. Repeat the corn cake, crème fraîche, and salmon layering until you have 3 layers. Sprinkle about 1/4 cup of the tomatoes around each corn cake. Slice the basil into very fine strips and sprinkle on the cakes. Serve immediately.

Corn Cakes

3/4 cup yellow cornmeal

1/2 teaspoon kosher salt

2 tablespoons all-purpose flour

1 tablespoon sugar

2 tablespoons unsalted butter

1 cup buttermilk

1 egg, lightly beaten

12 ounces Pacific salmon fillet, cut into 12 (1 by 2-inch by 1/2-inch-thick) pieces

Kosher salt and freshly ground black pepper

2 tablespoons olive oil

1 cup peeled, seeded, and diced heirloom tomatoes (1 to 2 tomatoes)

1/2 teaspoon freshly squeezed lemon juice

1/4 cup crème fraîche (page 112)

12 large fresh basil leaves

Dungeness Crab and Spinach Frittata

½ pound baby spinach leaves

2 tablespoons olive oil

1 cup very thinly sliced yellow onion

½ pound Yukon gold potatoes (about 2 potatoes), cut into ½-inch dice

Kosher salt and freshly ground white pepper

½ cup plain yogurt

½ cup heavy cream

10 eggs, beaten

Ground cayenne pepper

1 pound fresh Dungeness crabmeat, picked over for shell

1 bunch chives, thinly sliced

Each winter, I can hardly wait for northern California's Dungeness crab season to start, usually around the beginning of November. I put crab in just about anything, but especially enjoy it with the bright green color, mild flavor, and texture of spinach. In this recipe, the gentle flavors of eggs and spinach allow the crab to be the star. When you are cooking a green vegetable, such as spinach, the salt in the cooking water helps to keep the color bright. By immediately plunging the cooked spinach into ice water, you stop the cooking and retain the color. Another method to preserve color without using an ice bath is to coat the vegetable with olive oil and sprinkle with a little salt immediately after cooking. I like to serve frittatas for brunch, when Champagne is always welcome and usually demanded! You can serve this frittata at room temperature as well as straight out of the oven. KJ

Preheat the oven to 350°F. Butter a 1½-quart shallow baking dish.

Bring a pot of heavily salted water to a boil; the water should actually taste salty. Fill a large bowl with ice water. Plunge the spinach into the boiling water until just wilted, just a few seconds. Immediately remove from the boiling water with a slotted spoon and plunge into the ice water. Immediately remove from the ice water with a slotted spoon and place in a clean kitchen towel. Gently squeeze out as much water as you can. Transfer to a cutting board and chop coarsely.

Heat a large, nonstick sauté pan over medium-high heat and add the olive oil. When the oil is hot, add the onion and potatoes, season with salt and pepper, and cover. Decrease the heat to medium and cook, stirring often, for about 15 minutes, until the potatoes are soft on the inside and caramelized on the outside.

In a large bowl, combine the yogurt and cream and mix thoroughly. Add the eggs and mix well. Season with salt and cayenne pepper. Add the spinach, potatoes, crab, and chives and gently fold together. Pour into the prepared baking dish and place on the middle rack of the oven. Cook until just set in the middle, about 35 minutes.

To serve, place on the table with a large spoon and let your guests help themselves.

Crab Quesadillas with Jicama, Avocado, and Tomato Salsa

This is a great late summer or early fall dish, when tomatoes are at their peak. I look for interesting textures as well as flavors when creating recipes. Although very mild in flavor, the jicama adds a great crunchy texture that contrasts nicely with the smooth avocado in these quesadillas. The salsa also lends bite, acidity, and a little heat. Together, the ingredients create a balance. I like to experiment with different vegetables in the mix, including corn, peppers, chiles, and spinach. You can substitute cooked shrimp, lobster, or crayfish for the crabmeat (or even smoked chicken!). You can't go wrong in my book serving a Rosé Champagne, or any fruity white wine. KJ

2 cups diced jicama

2 tablespoons freshly squeezed lime juice

Kosher salt and freshly ground black pepper

Pinch of ground cayenne pepper

2 cups diced tomato (about 1 large tomato)

¼ cup minced jalapeño chile, seeded

1 tablespoon minced garlic

1 large avocado

8 (10-inch) flour tortillas

10 ounces Monterey Jack cheese, grated

½ pound fresh king, blue, or Dungeness crabmeat, picked over for shell

½ cup unsalted butter

In a small bowl, combine the jicama and lime juice and season with salt, pepper, and cayenne. In another small bowl, combine the tomato, jalapeño, and garlic and season with salt and pepper. Using a sharp paring knife, cut the avocado in half lengthwise and remove the pit. While still unpeeled, cut the flesh of both halves into a ¼-inch cross-hatch pattern without cutting through the skin.

Lay out 4 tortillas on a clean flat surface. Sprinkle half of the cheese on the tortillas. Evenly divide the jicama mixture and sprinkle on top of the cheese. Evenly divide the crab and sprinkle over the jicama. Evenly divide the tomato mixture and sprinkle over the crab. Spoon the avocado meat out of the skin, evenly divide, and sprinkle over the tomatoes. Sprinkle the remaining cheese over the avocado and top each with another tortilla. Lightly press down on the top tortillas.

Heat a large nonstick pan over medium-high heat and add 1 tablespoon of the butter. When the butter is melted, add 1 of the assembled quesadillas. Top with another 1 tablespoon of the butter. Cook until the underside is golden brown, about 3 minutes. Carefully turn the quesadilla over and cook the other side until golden brown, about 3 minutes. Remove from the pan and cut into 12 wedges. Repeat with the remaining quesadillas and butter. (You could use multiple pans if you want the cooking to go quicker.) Serve immediately.

Wild Mushroom Tart with Sweet Potatoes and Field Greens

2 recipes cornmeal tart dough
   (page 111)

1 cup heavy cream

2 extra large eggs, lightly whipped

1 tablespoon freshly grated
   Parmesan cheese

1½ teaspoons Dijon mustard

1 teaspoon freshly squeezed
   lemon juice

1 teaspoon finely grated lemon zest

Kosher salt and freshly ground
   black pepper

¼ pound mixed fresh wild mushrooms,
   such as chanterelle, hedgehog,
   oyster, lobster, and morel, cleaned
   and sliced

1 small sweet potato, peeled and cut
   into ¼-inch dice (about ½ cup)

1 tablespoon olive oil

1 teaspoon balsamic vinegar

1 tablespoon extra virgin olive oil

¼ pound mixed field greens

The success of these tarts depends on the interplay of the three dominant flavors—the earthy, savory taste of wild mushrooms; the sweetness of sweet potatoes; and the acidity of lemon and the dressed greens. The combination brings out the best in each of the ingredients. I prefer to fill the tarts with the custard when they are already sitting on the oven rack. This technique, which also works when preparing custards or soufflés, avoids any spilling on the way to the oven. A fruity Pinot Noir, Syrah, or Petite Sirah are my favorites with this dish. KJ

Preheat the oven to 350°F.

On a lightly floured work surface, roll out the chilled dough to ¼ inch thick. Using a pastry cutter, cut the dough into four 5-inch rounds. Line four 4-inch tart pans with the dough rounds. Cover the inside of each tart shell with a double piece of aluminum foil. Bake until half cooked or slightly opaque, about 15 minutes. Remove from the oven, discard the foil, and transfer to wire racks to cool slightly. Maintain the oven heat at 350°F. Remove the tart shells from the pans, place on a baking sheet, and set aside.

While the tart shells are cooking, mix together the cream, eggs, cheese, and 1 teaspoon of the mustard in a bowl until well combined.

In another bowl, combine the lemon juice and zest. Season with salt and pepper. Add the mushrooms and sweet potato and toss well.

Heat a large, nonstick pan over high heat and add the olive oil. When the oil is hot, almost to smoking, add the mushrooms and sweet potato. Cook, stirring often, until light golden brown, 3 to 5 minutes. Divide the vegetable mixture evenly among the tart shells. Place the baking sheet with the tart shells on the oven rack. Pour the egg mixture over the vegetables, filling just to the top of the shells. Bake until the custard has set, about 25 minutes.

In a bowl, combine the vinegar and the remaining ½ teaspoon mustard. Slowly whisk in the extra virgin olive oil. Season with salt and pepper. Add the field greens and toss gently to coat.

To serve, divide the greens among 4 plates. As soon as the tarts come out of the oven, pop a tart onto each plate, and serve immediately.

Porcini and Potato Gratin

1 cup dried porcini mushrooms
(about 1 ounce)

¼ cup Chardonnay

2 tablespoons unsalted butter

4 cloves garlic, minced

2 cups heavy cream

6 Yukon gold potatoes
(about 1¾ pounds), peeled and
cut into ¼-inch slices

1 teaspoon kosher salt

½ teaspoon freshly ground
black pepper

¼ teaspoon ground nutmeg

⅓ cup coarsely grated Asiago cheese

During certain seasons, you may find a wide selection of fresh mushrooms at your market, but most groceries also carry an extensive variety of dried mushrooms year-round. When reconstituted with water or even wine, they add full robust flavors to recipes. I find their earthy, rich taste partners best with Pinot Noirs, Syrahs, and Zinfandels. You can substitute dried shiitake mushrooms (stems trimmed) for the porcini and achieve a very similar result. For a slightly different flavor element, you could use blue cheese in place of the Asiago. GW

Place the dried mushrooms in a 2-cup measuring cup. Add the wine and fill with enough warm water to measure 2 cups of liquid. Let the mushrooms soak for 20 minutes, or until they become full and soft. Remove the mushrooms from the liquid and pass the liquid through a fine-meshed sieve to remove any dirt. Reserve ⅓ cup of the liquid. Rinse the mushrooms to remove any remaining sediment.

Preheat the oven to 400°F. Lightly oil an 8 by 8-inch shallow baking dish.

Heat a large sauté pan over medium heat and add the butter. When the butter is melted, add the garlic and sauté for 2 to 3 minutes, until tender. Add the mushrooms, reserved mushroom liquid, and cream and stir well. Add the potatoes, salt, pepper, and nutmeg. Bring to a boil, decrease the heat, and simmer for about 5 minutes, until heated through. Pour the mixture into the prepared baking dish and sprinkle evenly with the cheese. Bake for 25 minutes, or until lightly browned on top and the potatoes are tender. Serve immediately.

Blue Cheese and Garden Tomato Galette

Galettes are endlessly versatile; the inspiration for toppings can come from seasonal ingredients and your own preferences. This recipe is a great place to start. To make the dish heartier, try adding shrimp or ¼-inch slices of sausage. Another variation could be a mix of your favorite cheese and herbs combined with fresh corn kernels and thinly sliced zucchini. I find it easy to double the dough recipe and freeze one disk for up to two months. Remove the dough from the freezer one day ahead and place it in the refrigerator to thaw. Recommended wines are based on your choice of ingredients. Pinot Noir or Merlot work well with this recipe because their medium body and fruit characteristics complement the dominant tomato and cheese flavors. GW

2 to 3 tomatoes, thinly sliced

2 tablespoons olive oil

1 large Vidalia or other sweet onion, thinly sliced

4 cloves garlic, minced

¼ cup chopped fresh basil

1 teaspoon finely chopped fresh oregano

1 teaspoon finely chopped fresh tarragon

1 recipe cornmeal tart dough (page 111)

½ cup crumbled mild blue cheese

Kosher salt and freshly ground black pepper

1 egg white, lightly beaten

Place the rack in the center of the oven and preheat to 375°F. Lay the sliced tomatoes on paper towels to absorb some of the liquid.

Heat a sauté pan over medium heat and add the olive oil. When the oil is hot, add the onion and garlic and sauté, stirring frequently, until lightly browned, 8 to 10 minutes. Add the basil, oregano, and tarragon and stir well. Remove from the heat and set aside to cool.

Line a baking sheet with parchment paper. On a floured work surface, roll out the dough to a round 15 inches in diameter and about ⅛ inch thick. Trim off any rough edges. Roll the dough over the rolling pin and transfer to the prepared baking sheet. Spread the cheese evenly over the dough, leaving a 2-inch uncovered border around the edges. Spread the onion mixture over the cheese. Overlap the tomatoes on top of the onion mixture. Season with salt and pepper. Fold the border of the dough up over the filling toward the center, pleating every couple of inches to form a crust. Repair any tears by pinching the dough together. With a pastry brush, gently paint the pleated edges of the dough with the egg white.

Bake for 35 minutes, or until the crust is browned and the filling is bubbling. Allow to cool for 5 to 10 minutes before cutting into wedges and serving.

Butternut Squash and Goat Cheese Gratin

8 ounces fresh goat cheese,
   at room temperature

¾ cup milk

1 (1½- to 2-pound) butternut squash,
   peeled, seeded, and very thinly
   sliced (about 4 cups)

Kosher salt and freshly ground
   black pepper

2 cups fresh bread crumbs
   (page 110)

1 tablespoon finely chopped
   fresh thyme

⅓ cup freshly grated Parmigiano-
   Reggiano cheese

This is a wonderful side dish for Thanksgiving. Butternut squash has a sweet, pumpkin-like flavor that is a perfect foil for the tartness and creamy texture of goat cheese. You can change the flavors in this recipe by using different herbs such as sage, oregano, or marjoram. Fresh ginger can also be a tasty addition that pairs very nicely with the squash; add 2 tablespoons grated ginger along with the herbs. Since this is a side dish, look to the main dish's dominant flavors when pairing a wine. On its own, this recipe would pair well with a Riesling or a Gewürztraminer. *KJ*

Preheat the oven to 350°F.

In a bowl, whisk together the goat cheese and milk until smooth. Add the squash and toss to coat lightly. Season with salt and pepper. Arrange the squash in layers in a shallow 2-quart baking dish. Pour in any remaining liquid from the bowl.

In a small bowl, combine the bread crumbs, thyme, and cheese. Sprinkle evenly over the squash. Place in the oven and bake until the squash is easily pierced with a sharp knife, 50 to 60 minutes. The top of the gratin may get browned before the squash is cooked through. If this happens, cover with a piece of aluminum foil so the bread crumbs don't burn. Remove from the oven and serve warm.

Summer Vegetable Risotto with Truffle Oil

Serves 4

I always keep chicken stock and risotto rice on hand for a last-minute quick supper, with any available vegetables thrown in. I like to partially cook the vegetables in the pan in the beginning, remove them, and add them back in at the end. This incorporates their flavors into the risotto while preserving their texture. My favorite wine with this dish is Pinot Noir, but I have enjoyed it with Chardonnay and Sauvignon Blanc as well. KJ

Bring the stock to a boil in a saucepan over high heat. Decrease the heat to maintain a simmer. Heat a thick-bottomed pot over medium heat and add the olive oil. When the oil is hot, add the shallots, squash, zucchini, corn, and spring onion and cook until translucent, about 5 minutes. Remove the vegetables from the pot and set aside. Add the rice to the pot. Cook, stirring often, until the rice is coated with the oil and starts to change color but is not browning. The rice should just start sticking to the bottom of the pot and make a little squealing sound. Season with a little salt.

Using a ladle, add enough hot stock to cover the rice by about ½ inch. Decrease the heat to medium-low and cook, stirring often with a wooden spoon, until most of the stock is absorbed, 5 to 10 minutes. Continue to add stock in ¾-cup amounts, stirring each addition until the liquid is almost all absorbed before adding the next. The stock should always be barely simmering, and be careful to not let the rice get too dry. Taste as you go to ensure that the rice is cooked to your liking; I prefer risotto with a little crunch, but still cooked through. You need to add enough stock in the final phases of cooking so that a nice, medium-thick sauce forms. The total cooking time will be 30 to 35 minutes. Add the garlic and cooked vegetables when the last addition of liquid is almost absorbed, and mix thoroughly.

When the rice is cooked and the vegetables are warmed through, stir in the truffle oil, cheese, tarragon, and lemon juice. Taste and adjust the seasoning with salt and pepper if necessary. Add one final ladleful of stock, cover, and let sit for a few minutes. Divide among 4 bowls and serve immediately.

About 4 cups chicken stock (page 111)

1 tablespoon olive oil

1 tablespoon minced shallots

¼ cup finely diced summer squash

¼ cup finely diced zucchini

½ cup fresh corn kernels (about 1 ear)

¼ cup chopped spring onion, including white and green parts

1 cup Carnaroli or Arborio rice

Kosher salt

1 teaspoon minced garlic

1 tablespoon truffle oil

¼ cup freshly grated Parmesan cheese

1 teaspoon minced fresh tarragon

2 teaspoons freshly squeezed lemon juice

Freshly ground black pepper

Breakfast Pizza with Prosciutto, Egg, Tomato, and Squash

Pizza for breakfast? Why not! This is really just ham and eggs done in a less traditional manner. If the egg is not quite finished cooking but the dough is golden brown, you can slip the pizza under your broiler until it's done (it won't take long). This same style of breakfast pizza can also be made using smoked salmon, sautéed spinach, or any number of ingredient combinations. If you can't find a citrus-flavored oil, you can make it yourself by adding a pinch of grated citrus zest to 1 tablespoon extra virgin olive oil. KJ

Prepare the oven for pizza baking as described on page 117; preheat it to 500°F.

Heat a sauté pan over high heat and add the olive oil. When the oil is hot, add the squash. Remove from the heat and toss in the pan for 30 seconds, until slightly browned. In a bowl, combine the squash, tomatoes, chervil, and parsley and season with salt and pepper.

With flour-dusted hands, stretch and shape each piece of dough into a 10-inch round or roll out with a rolling pin. For each pizza, cover the dough with one-fourth of the prosciutto, leaving a 1 1/2-inch uncovered border around the edges. Spread one-fourth of the vegetables over the prosciutto and sprinkle with 1 teaspoon of the Parmesan. Fold the border of the dough up over the filling, pleating every couple of inches (like a galette). Crack an egg onto the middle of the pizza.

Slide the pizzas onto the pizza stone or a baking sheet in the oven and bake until the dough is golden brown and the egg has set, 6 to 8 minutes. Depending on the size of your pizza stone, you may have to do these in a couple of batches. When each pizza is done, place it on a plate, drizzle with a little Meyer lemon oil, and serve immediately.

2 tablespoons olive oil

2 summer, crookneck, or zucchini squash, cut into 1/4-inch dice

2 tomatoes, peeled, seeded, and diced

2 teaspoons chopped fresh chervil or tarragon

1 teaspoon chopped fresh flat-leaf parsley

Kosher salt and freshly ground black pepper

1/2 recipe pizza dough, divided into 4 pieces (page 114)

4 ounces prosciutto, very thinly sliced

1 tablespoon plus 1 teaspoon finely grated Parmesan cheese

4 extra large eggs

1 teaspoon Meyer lemon oil (or any citrus-flavored oil)

Plum Coffee Cake

1 cup sugar

1 cup walnuts, pecans, or
almonds, ground

1 teaspoon ground cinnamon

1 teaspoon ground nutmeg

3 tablespoons unsalted butter,
at room temperature

1½ cups all-purpose flour

2 teaspoons baking powder

½ teaspoon kosher salt

1 egg

⅔ cup buttermilk

¼ cup unsalted butter, melted
and cooled

5 ripe plums, cut into ¼-inch slices

During the summer when my grandmother's plum trees were hanging with ripened fruit, we would get up early in the morning and pick a few to make this coffee cake. Its simplicity and freshness on a summer morning cannot be beat. Try pluots or nectarines as an alternative fruit. You can also serve this as a dessert with French vanilla bean or lemon ice cream. When you serve as a dessert, try it with a glass of Late Harvest Riesling. GW

Preheat the oven to 350°F. Butter and flour an 8 by 8-inch baking dish.

In a small bowl, combine ¼ cup of the sugar, the ground nuts, cinnamon, and nutmeg. With your fingers, add the softened butter and work it into the mixture with your fingers until it resembles a coarse crumble.

In a small bowl, combine the flour, baking powder, and salt. In a separate bowl, combine the egg and remaining ¾ cup sugar and blend with an electric mixer on medium speed until smooth. Pour in the buttermilk and mix thoroughly. Add the flour mixture, blend until just smooth, then slowly add the melted butter. Blend until well mixed, 2 to 3 minutes. Pour the batter into the prepared baking dish. Gently arrange the plum slices on top of the batter in rows.

Sprinkle the nut mixture evenly over the plums. Bake for about 30 minutes, until a toothpick inserted into the center comes out clean. Remove from the oven and allow to cool for 10 minutes. Cut into squares and serve warm or at room temperature.

Zinfandel Barbecue Sauce

Zinfandel is my barbecue wine. It has a wonderful affinity for grilled meats, poultry, and even salmon. I especially like Zinfandels that are fruity, bordering on sweet, for this sauce. Brush the sauce on at the end of cooking to prevent burning, or serve as a dipping sauce on the side. I would serve the same wine that I used to make the sauce with the meal. *KJ*

3 cups whole peeled canned tomatoes, with juice

1 tablespoon olive oil

½ yellow onion, diced

1 tablespoon chopped garlic

¾ cup plus 1 tablespoon Zinfandel

¼ cup plus 2 tablespoons red wine vinegar

1½ cups ketchup

3 tablespoons chopped canned chipotle chiles in adobo sauce, seeds removed

2½ tablespoons Worcestershire sauce

¼ cup firmly packed light brown sugar

2 tablespoons maple syrup

Place a strainer over a bowl and pour the canned tomatoes into the strainer. Seed the tomatoes over the strainer so the strainer catches the seeds, then add the tomatoes to the bowl of juice. Discard the seeds and set the tomatoes and juice aside.

Heat a sauté pan over medium heat and add the oil. When the oil is hot, add the onion and sauté, stirring often, until almost caramelized, about 10 minutes. Add the garlic and cook for about 2 minutes, continuing to stir. Add the wine and vinegar and scrape any toasted bits from the bottom of the pan. Stir in the tomatoes and juice, ketchup, chiles with the sauce, Worcestershire, brown sugar, and syrup and bring to a boil. Decrease the heat to low and simmer, stirring occasionally to ensure that the bottom is not burning, for 2 to 3 hours. In batches, transfer to a blender and purée until smooth. Transfer to a bowl and allow to cool until ready to use. The sauce can be stored in an airtight container in the refrigerator for up to 1 month.

Big Bites

Whether it's fish, fowl, meat, pasta, or vegetarian fare, the following recipes set the tenor for larger meals. In these pages, you can find . . .

A balanced recipe to go with a special wine

A complete meal—an entrée and a complementary side dish

A place to start when planning a dinner party

Something to accompany a favorite side dish

A quick dinner solution

Grilled Summer Vegetable Ratatouille

1 large eggplant, cut lengthwise into
¼-inch-thick slices

Kosher salt

6 tablespoons olive oil

¼ cup dry white wine

1 teaspoon finely chopped fresh thyme

1 teaspoon finely chopped
fresh oregano

1 teaspoon finely chopped
fresh rosemary

Juice of 1 lemon

4 yellow crookneck squash, cut
lengthwise into ¼-inch slices

4 zucchini, cut into ¼-inch rounds

3 cloves garlic, minced

1½ cups chopped yellow onion

1 large green bell pepper, diced

1 large yellow bell pepper, diced

3 cups peeled, seeded, and coarsely
chopped fresh tomatoes (3 to 4
tomatoes)

1 cup fresh mushrooms, cut into
⅛-inch slices

Freshly ground black pepper

½ cup freshly shredded Parmigiano-
Reggiano cheese

2 tablespoons chopped fresh flat-leaf
parsley, for garnish

Among really useful grilling tools—a good pair of long-handled, spring-loaded tongs; a large spatula; hot pads; a long-handled pastry brush; and an instant-read thermometer—I also rank a grill basket. I use it frequently for grilling all kinds of vegetables and fruit as it prevents smaller pieces from falling into the fire. You'll find one very handy when making this dish. For a meatless supper, try this recipe over toasted country bread with a glass of Sauvignon Blanc. If you have any ratatouille left over, it is terrific served cold the next day as a side dish. GW

Place the eggplant on paper towels in a single layer, salt lightly, and let sit for 20 minutes. Pat dry with paper towels.

Prepare a medium-hot fire in a charcoal grill or preheat a gas grill to medium-high.

In a large bowl, whisk together ¼ cup of the olive oil, the wine, thyme, oregano, rosemary, and lemon juice to make a marinade. Add the eggplant, squash, and zucchini to the marinade and lightly toss to coat evenly. Spread the vegetables evenly in the bottom of a large grill basket. (You may have to do this in a couple of batches to prevent overcrowding.) Reserve the marinade for basting.

Place the basket on the grill rack and grill for 3 to 4 minutes, then baste the vegetables with the marinade. Turn all the vegetables and grill for 3 to 4 minutes, until tender but not overcooked. Remove the basket from the grill and set aside. When the vegetables are cool enough to handle, transfer to a cutting board, and chop the eggplant and crookneck squash into 1½-inch pieces.

Heat a large sauté pan over medium heat and add the remaining 2 tablespoons oil. When the oil is hot, add the garlic and onion and sauté until soft but not browned, 3 to 5 minutes. Add the bell peppers and continue to sauté until tender, 3 to 5 minutes. Add the tomatoes and mushrooms and season with salt and pepper. Simmer until the tomato and mushroom juices have evaporated, about 15 minutes. Add the grilled vegetables, stir well, and cover. Simmer until the grilled vegetables are heated through, 5 to 7 minutes. Remove from the heat and transfer to a serving dish. Sprinkle with the cheese, garnish with the parsley, and serve immediately.

Portobello Mushroom Sandwich with Roasted Peppers, Fennel, and Lime Aioli

The juicy, earthy flavor of cooked portobello mushrooms is a wonderful alternative to a burger or other meat-filled sandwiches. The fennel brings an anise note and provides some crunchy texture, while the peppers add a little sweetness. The tart lime aioli helps to accentuate the other ingredients. I have served these mushrooms as a vegetarian main course for dinner guests who do not eat meat. (With my friends, usually one eats meat, the other doesn't!) I especially like the earthiness of a Pinot Noir or Syrah with this sandwich. KJ

Preheat the oven to 375°F.

In a bowl, combine the mushrooms, garlic, vinegar, and the 2 tablespoons olive oil. Toss gently and season with salt and pepper. Place, top sides up, on a baking sheet and slide into the oven. Cook for about 12 minutes, turn over, and cook on the other side for about 10 minutes. The mushrooms should be lightly browned and cooked through. Remove from the oven and allow to cool.

Roast the peppers over an open flame or in a broiler until lightly blackened on all sides. Place in a bowl and cover with plastic wrap to steam for about 5 minutes. (This will ease the skinning process.) Remove the skins from the peppers and trim off the stem and bottom. Cut each pepper in half and remove the ribs and seeds.

In a small bowl, combine the lemon juice and the 2 teaspoons olive oil. Season with salt and pepper. Add the peppers and fennel and toss well.

Split the buns in half and toast them lightly. Spread aioli on both sides of the buns. Layer a mushroom, half a roasted pepper, one-fourth of the fennel, and 1/2 cup of the lettuce on the bottom half of each bun. Cover each with a bun top and cut the sandwiches in half. Serve immediately.

4 large portobello mushrooms, stems and gills removed

1 teaspoon minced garlic

1 tablespoon balsamic vinegar

2 tablespoons plus 2 teaspoons extra virgin olive oil

Kosher salt and freshly ground black pepper

2 red bell peppers

1 teaspoon freshly squeezed lemon juice

1 small head fennel, thinly sliced

4 large hamburger buns

1 cup aioli, made with lime juice in place of lemon juice (page 110)

2 cups baby lettuces

Shrimp with Blood Oranges and Skillet Polenta

1 cup dry white wine

1 cup freshly squeezed
blood orange juice

1 tablespoon chopped garlic

1 tablespoon chopped fresh dill

24 large (21 to 25 count) shrimp,
shelled and deveined

Polenta

6 cups cold water

1 teaspoon kosher salt

1 cup polenta or coarse cornmeal

¼ cup unsalted butter, cut into
½-inch pieces

¾ cup freshly grated Romano cheese

Kosher salt and freshly ground
black pepper

2 tablespoons olive oil

3 tablespoons minced shallots

2 tablespoons grated peeled
fresh ginger

16 blood orange sections, membranes
removed (about 2 oranges)

2 tablespoons coarsely chopped fresh
flat-leaf parsley

1 tablespoon unsalted butter

1 tablespoon finely grated
blood orange zest, for garnish

The lively flavor of shrimp marinated in orange juice, wine, and dill provides a perfect foil for creamy, cheesy polenta in this memorable entrée. These large shrimp are classified at 21 to 25 per pound, with the cost per pound generally higher for the larger sizes. You can substitute smaller-sized shrimp, but you will need to increase the number of shrimp accordingly and slightly decrease the cooking time. I like the size of larger shrimp and find them easier to shell. To maximize your time while you are preparing this recipe, start with shelling and marinating the shrimp. Then make the polenta and, while it is setting in the refrigerator, prepare the ingredients for cooking the shrimp. This allows you to finish the polenta while sautéing the shrimp so everything will come together at once. I prefer white wine with this recipe and several varietals will work nicely. Try some full-flavored Sauvignon Blancs with lots of citrus character to balance with the blood oranges. On the lighter side, a Pinot Grigio or crisp, dry Gewürztraminer are also among my favorites. GW

In a bowl, combine the wine, ½ cup of the orange juice, garlic, and dill. Add the shrimp and lightly toss to coat evenly. Set aside in the refrigerator for at least 1 hour or up to 6 hours.

To prepare the polenta, in a large saucepan over medium-high heat, combine the water and salt and bring to a boil. Slowly stir in the polenta, decrease the heat, and simmer gently, stirring frequently and scraping the sides and bottom of the pan to prevent sticking. Cook for 30 minutes, or until the polenta loses its grainy texture and becomes thick and smooth. If the polenta begins to thicken too quickly before it is fully cooked, add a little more water and continue to stir until done. Stir in the butter and ½ cup of the cheese and continue to mix until melted and blended together. Taste and adjust the seasoning with salt if necessary. Oil a cast-iron skillet or an ovenproof sauté pan. Pour the polenta into the skillet and place in the refrigerator to cool and firm, about 30 minutes.

When the polenta is firm, preheat the broiler. Remove the skillet from the refrigerator and place over medium-low heat for about 10 minutes, until the polenta is almost heated through. Sprinkle the top with the remaining ¼ cup cheese and slip under the broiler. Broil until the cheese melts and the top is golden brown, about 5 minutes. Remove from the broiler and cut into wedges.

Drain the shrimp, discarding the marinade, and season with salt and pepper. Heat a large sauté pan over medium-high heat and add the olive oil. When the oil is hot, add the shallots and ginger and sauté for 2 minutes, until golden. Add the shrimp and sauté for 3 minutes on each side, or until bright pink. Remove the pan from the heat, add the orange sections and 1 tablespoon of the parsley, and toss well.

To serve, divide the shrimp and blood oranges among 4 plates. Place the sauté pan over medium-high heat, add the remaining $^1/_2$ cup blood orange juice and the butter, and scrape the toasted bits off the bottom of the pan. Heat for 3 to 4 minutes, until simmering and the butter has melted. Taste and adjust the seasoning if necessary. Drizzle the sauce over the shrimp on each plate. Add 1 to 2 polenta wedges to each plate and garnish with the remaining 1 tablespoon parsley and the orange zest. Serve immediately.

Potato-Crusted Sea Bass with Gingered Blue Lake Beans

Serves 4

2 large russet potatoes, peeled

4 cups peanut oil, for deep-frying

Kosher salt

4 (1-inch-thick) sea bass fillets
(1¼ to 1½ pounds total)

1 tablespoon olive oil

1 tablespoon minced fresh chives

1 tablespoon minced fresh
flat-leaf parsley

2 tablespoons minced fresh chervil
or thyme

Freshly ground black pepper

1 pound Blue Lake green beans,
ends trimmed

¼ cup unsalted butter

2 tablespoons finely chopped peeled
fresh ginger

Juice of 1 lemon

2 tablespoons chopped fresh
flat-leaf parsley

Surprising things may happen when you prepare this dish. One of our recipe testers had enlisted the help of her sixteen-year-old grandson, an avowed "no fish" eater. After eating every morsel, way beyond the required taste, he declared it deserved our highest rating. This recipe may look complicated but is really very easy and is a quick, fun way to serve fish. You can substitute other thick white fish such as grouper or halibut.

I enjoy a fuller-bodied Chardonnay with this dish (particularly while I am cooking it!) as it matches the weight and flavor of the potatoes and fish. The ginger gives a bit of spice, which can be moderated by a rich Chardonnay. A Sauvignon Blanc works well too, particularly if it is on the medium-bodied side. GW

To prepare the crust, julienne the potatoes into $^1/_{16}$-inch strips with a mandoline or in a food processor. As the potatoes are cut, place them in cold water to prevent browning. When finished cutting, drain the potatoes and pat dry with paper towels.

Place a large, deep sauté pan over high heat and pour in the peanut oil to a depth of about 2 inches. The oil is ready for frying when a piece of potato sizzles when dropped into it. Add the potatoes in batches, frying for 6 to 8 minutes, until golden brown. Carefully remove the potatoes with a slotted spoon and place on paper towels to drain. Sprinkle with salt to taste. Allow the potatoes to cool for about 5 minutes, then coarsely chop them.

Preheat the oven to 375°F. Lightly brush both sides of the fish fillets with the olive oil. In a small bowl, mix together the chives, minced parsley, and chervil and season with salt and pepper. Reserve about 1 teaspoon of the herb mixture for a final garnish. Coat the fish on both sides with the herb mixture. With your fingers, press the potatoes on the top side of each fillet, forming a crust. Lightly oil a baking dish and add the coated fillets, crust side up. Bake for 10 to 12 minutes for medium doneness, until the fish is flaky but still moist inside and the crust is crisp and golden.

(continued)

While the fish is baking, cover the bottom of a large sauté pan with about ¹/₄ inch of cold water, add the beans, and sprinkle with salt to taste. Cover and bring to a boil over high heat. Decrease the heat to achieve a simmer and cook the beans for about 2 minutes, until brilliant green. Drain immediately in a colander. The beans should still be very crisp. Add the butter and ginger to the same sauté pan over medium-high heat. Sauté the ginger for 2 to 3 minutes, until fragrant but not browned. Add the beans and toss to coat well. Add the lemon juice and chopped parsley and toss lightly. Taste and adjust the seasoning with salt and pepper if necessary.

To serve, place a piece of fish in the center of each plate and surround with the beans. Garnish the fish and beans with the reserved herb mixture and serve immediately.

Shrimp Linguine with Tomatoes, Almonds, and Chile

Serves 4

The inspiration for this pasta finds its roots in the Spanish romesco sauce, a spicy blend of chile, garlic, tomato, and almonds usually served with shrimp. The almonds help to slightly thicken the sauce, adding texture as well as flavor. We drink Sauvignon Blanc as our house wine and I love cooking with it. Because most Sauvignon Blancs are made in a clean, straightforward style without any oak aging, they work well as an ingredient; they don't dominate the flavors in the dish. Most other dry white wines, such as Pinot Grigio, Riesling, or Viognier, can also be paired with this pasta. KJ

Peel and devein the shrimp, reserving the shells. In a bowl, combine the chile powder and cayenne. Add the shrimp and toss to coat evenly. Season with salt and pepper. Use right away or set aside in the refrigerator for up to 1 hour.

Drain the liquid from the tomatoes into a bowl. Place a strainer over the bowl, cut the tomatoes in half, and remove the seeds over the strainer to catch the juice. Coarsely chop the tomatoes and reserve. Heat a large nonreactive sauté pan over medium-high heat. Add the shrimp shells and cook, stirring often, until golden, about 5 minutes. Add the wine and the juice from the tomatoes. Cook, uncovered, until slightly thickened, about 15 minutes. Pass through a medium-meshed sieve, discarding the shells and reserving the liquid.

Bring a large pot of salted water to a boil over high heat. Add the pasta and cook according to the package instructions, until al dente.

While the pasta is cooking, heat a large nonreactive pan over high heat and add the olive oil. When the oil is hot, add the shrimp and sauté until lightly golden and cooked about halfway through, about 1 1/2 minutes on each side. The shrimp should still be a little rare on the inside. Add the garlic and cook for 1 minute, stirring constantly. Add the reserved tomato juice mixture, tomatoes, and almonds and cook for about 2 minutes, until the shrimp are cooked through. Add lemon juice, salt, and pepper to taste.

Drain the pasta when done and toss in the pan with the shrimp mixture. Taste and adjust the seasoning with salt, pepper, and lemon juice if necessary. Divide among 4 plates and serve immediately.

1 pound extra large (16 to 20 count) shrimp

1 teaspoon chile powder

1/8 teaspoon ground cayenne pepper

Kosher salt and freshly ground black pepper

1 (28-ounce) can whole tomatoes in juice

1 cup dry white wine, such as Sauvignon Blanc

3/4 pound dried linguine

1 tablespoon olive oil

1 teaspoon minced garlic

1/2 cup toasted and finely ground almonds (page 118)

About 1 teaspoon freshly squeezed lemon juice

Vermouth-Steamed Mahi-Mahi en Papillote

Serves 4

Spicy Dipping Sauce

3 tablespoons rice wine vinegar

3 tablespoons soy sauce

3 tablespoons sake

2 tablespoons mirin

½ teaspoon sesame oil

¼ teaspoon chile-garlic sauce

¾ teaspoon fine sugar

4 teaspoons finely chopped peeled
   fresh ginger

Nutty Dipping Sauce

2 tablespoons sake

2 tablespoons mirin

2 tablespoons light brown or
   yellow miso

2 tablespoons soy sauce

2 tablespoons finely chopped peeled
   fresh ginger

4 (4- to 6-ounce) mahi-mahi fillets

¼ cup freshly squeezed lemon juice

2 teaspoons finely grated lemon zest

Kosher salt and freshly ground
   black pepper

¼ cup dry vermouth

2 tablespoons coarsely chopped fresh
   chervil, flat-leaf parsley, or shiso

½ yellow bell pepper, cut into
   2-inch julienne

3 green onions, white part only,
   cut into 2-inch julienne

½ jalapeño chile, seeded and cut into
   2-inch julienne

A dry white wine, Lillet (a French apéritif), or sake can be used in place of the vermouth for steaming. The subtle taste and aroma of the fish will change slightly, reflecting the flavors in the steaming liquid. If mahi-mahi is not available, sea bass and halibut are great alternatives. You will need four 15-inch-square pieces of parchment paper and a straw to make the papillotes. Our friend Moaya Schieman tested this recipe and provided some wonderful adjustments, as well as the two dipping sauces. Enjoy this dish with a crisp white wine such as a Pinot Blanc or Sauvignon Blanc, and when serving a red wine, a Beaujolais or Pinot Noir. GW

Preheat the oven to 400°F.

To prepare the dipping sauces, combine all the ingredients for each in 2 separate, small saucepans over high heat. Bring to a boil, decrease the heat to low, and simmer for 2 minutes. Remove from the heat and set aside to allow the flavors to marry and develop.

To prepare the mahi-mahi, cut four 15-inch pieces of parchment paper and fold each in half. Place 1 fillet on each piece, next to the fold. Evenly sprinkle each fillet with 1 tablespoon of the lemon juice and ½ teaspoon of the zest. Season with salt and pepper. Sprinkle each with 1 tablespoon of the vermouth and one-fourth of the chervil. Top each with one-fourth of the julienned bell pepper, onion, and jalapeño.

Fold the paper halves together, then tightly crimp the edges to seal each packet completely. Just before you make the last crimp, inflate the papillote by gently blowing it up with a straw. Quickly remove the straw and double-fold to seal in the air. Place the papillotes on a baking sheet and bake for 15 minutes, until the paper browns slightly.

To serve, carefully place each papillote on a dinner plate. Cut an **X** in the paper and fold back the edges to reveal the fish. Divide each dipping sauce among 4 small bowls and place a bowl of each beside each plate. Serve immediately.

Capellini with Lemon, Capers, Herb Oil, and Smoked Trout

With the exception of the smoked trout, I usually seem to have these ingredients on hand in my house, which makes this an especially simple last-minute dish. The brightness of the herbs, lemon, and capers is a pleasant contrast to the trout's smoky flavors (almost any smoked fish could be substituted). Be careful when seasoning with salt as the capers and smoked fish are already salted. Any dry, crisp white wine is great with this dish but my favorites are Sauvignon Blanc, Pinot Blanc, or Pinot Grigio. KJ

To prepare the herb oil, combine the parsley, basil, and olive oil in a mini blender and process until smooth. Transfer to a small bowl and stir in the extra virgin olive oil, cheese, and garlic. Season with salt and pepper.

Bring a large pot of salted water to a boil over high heat. Add the pasta and cook according to the package instructions, or until al dente. Drain, transfer to a bowl, and toss with the lemon juice, zest, capers, and herb oil.

To serve, divide the pasta among 4 plates. Twist the pasta with a fork as you put it on the plates to get a nice tight nest with as much height as possible. Drizzle each plate with some of the oil and capers remaining in the bottom of the pasta bowl. Top with the smoked trout and garnish with the crème fraîche and chives. Serve immediately.

Herb Oil
¼ cup mixed fresh flat-leaf parsley and basil leaves

2 tablespoons olive oil

2 tablespoons extra virgin olive oil

1 tablespoon finely grated Parmigiano-Reggiano cheese

1 teaspoon minced garlic

Kosher salt and freshly ground black pepper

¾ pound fresh or dried capellini

Juice of 1 lemon

Finely grated zest of 1 lemon

1 tablespoon drained capers

½ pound smoked trout, flaked

1 tablespoon crème fraîche (page 112), for garnish

1 tablespoon minced fresh chives, for garnish

Grilled Halibut with Cauliflower-Leek Purée, Roasted Tomatoes, and Basil Oil

Serves 8 as a first course or
4 as a main course

The smoothness of the vegetable purée provides a nice contrast to the halibut's meaty texture. The addition of leeks to the purée helps to tone down the cauliflower's strong flavors, producing a more balanced and delicate accompaniment for the mild halibut. A vegetable stock or even milk can be used instead of the chicken stock if you want a vegetarian purée. This dish is great with medium-bodied wines such as Sauvignon Blanc, Chardonnay, and Merlot. KJ

Preheat the oven to 300°F.

Core the tomatoes and cut in half. Spread the garlic on the cut surfaces of the tomatoes, season with salt and pepper, and drizzle with the vinegar. Place on a baking sheet and roast for about 1 hour, until slightly dried out. Keep warm in a low-temperature oven.

Prepare a medium fire in a charcoal grill or preheat a gas grill to medium.

Heat the stock in a small, nonreactive stockpot over medium-high heat. Add the leek and cook until softened, about 5 minutes. Layer the cauliflower on top of the leek and sprinkle with a little salt. Decrease the heat, cover, and simmer gently until the cauliflower is soft, 10 to 15 minutes. Drain in a medium-meshed sieve, capturing the stock in a bowl. Purée the cauliflower and leek in a food processor until very smooth. If it is too thick to process, thin with a little of the reserved chicken stock. Return the purée to the pot. Taste and adjust the seasoning with salt, pepper, and a squeeze of lemon juice if necessary. Cover and keep warm over low heat.

To prepare the basil oil, quickly mince the basil. In a small bowl, combine the basil with the olive oil and parsley. Season with salt and pepper.

Season the halibut with salt and pepper and rub with extra virgin olive oil. Rub the grill rack down with the cut onion to clean it. Place the halibut on the rack, skin side down; the fat in the skin helps to season the grill. Cook, turning once, until still a little translucent inside, about 10 minutes. Be sure to wait until the fish starts to loosen from the grill before turning it; if it's sticking, it's not ready to be turned. If you prefer, you may remove the skin after cooking the fish.

To serve, spoon some cauliflower purée on each plate and place half a red tomato and half a yellow tomato alongside. Lean the halibut on the purée and drizzle with the basil oil. Serve immediately.

2 red tomatoes

2 yellow tomatoes

4 cloves garlic, thinly sliced

Kosher salt and freshly ground black pepper

1 tablespoon sherry vinegar

1 cup chicken stock (page 111)

1 large leek, white part only, julienned

1 head cauliflower, cored and separated into florets

Freshly squeezed lemon juice

¼ cup fresh basil leaves

¼ cup extra virgin olive oil, more for rubbing the fish

1 teaspoon minced fresh flat-leaf parsley

4 (6-ounce) halibut fillets, skin on

1 red onion, halved lengthwise

Red Snapper with Purple Basil Pesto and Citrus Basmati Rice

Citrus Basmati Rice

2 cups water

½ teaspoon kosher salt

1 cup brown basmati rice

½ cup raisins

½ cup dry sherry

⅓ cup freshly squeezed Meyer
   lemon juice

1 teaspoon kosher salt

½ teaspoon freshly ground
   black pepper

2 teaspoons ground cumin

2 teaspoons curry powder

1 teaspoon finely grated lemon zest

⅛ teaspoon Tabasco sauce

½ cup extra virgin olive oil

½ cup pistachios, toasted and skinned
   (page 118)

¼ cup chopped green onions,
   including white and green parts

Pesto

1½ cups loosely packed purple
   basil leaves

1 cup loosely packed cilantro leaves

2 tablespoons chopped garlic

1 teaspoon kosher salt

1 teaspoon freshly ground
   black pepper

½ cup extra virgin olive oil

½ cup freshly grated Parmigiano-
   Reggiano cheese

1 to 2 tablespoons olive oil

4 (6- to 7-ounce) fillets red snapper

Kosher salt and freshly ground
   black pepper

I use Meyer lemons to add a sparkling flavor to the rice, which complements this pan-fried red snapper. You can add other types of fresh lemon or orange juices to make the rice a great foil for the fish. The rice can be served warm or at room temperature, which makes it great to take on picnics too. The purple basil in the pesto adds a peppery and pungent flavor that I love to pair with Sauvignon Blanc. A crisp Chardonnay or Pinot Blanc would also match the lemon flavors and spices found in this dish. CW

To prepare the rice, in a saucepan over high heat, combine the water and salt, stir in the rice, and bring to a boil. Decrease the heat to low, stir once, and cover. Simmer for 40 minutes, or until the water is absorbed and the rice feels firm between the teeth, not crunchy or too soft.

Meanwhile, in a small bowl, combine the raisins and sherry. Let sit for 10 to 15 minutes, until the raisins are plumped. Drain.

In a small bowl, mix together the lemon juice, salt, pepper, cumin, curry, lemon zest, and Tabasco. Gradually whisk in the oil. Taste and adjust the seasoning with salt and pepper if necessary.

When the rice is cooked, remove from the heat and stir in the lemon juice mixture. Add the raisins, pistachios, and green onions, toss gently, cover, and keep warm.

To prepare the pesto, combine the basil, cilantro, garlic, salt, and pepper in a food processor. Pulse to blend. Continue to blend, adding the extra virgin olive oil in a thin stream, until smooth. By hand, add the cheese and stir until well mixed, scraping the sides as necessary.

Heat a large sauté pan over medium-high heat and add the olive oil. Season both sides of the snapper with salt and pepper. When the oil is hot, add the snapper and sauté, turning once, for 3 to 4 minutes on each side, until the fish just begins to flake with pressure from a fork.

To serve, place a piece of snapper in the center of each plate, spoon the rice around, and drizzle 2 tablespoons of pesto over the fish. Place the remaining pesto in a small serving bowl and pass at the table.

Bay Scallops with Rhubarb Purée

Serves 4

Bay scallops have a sweeter and richer flavor, smaller size, and crisper texture than sea scallops. If bay scallops are not available, you can cut up larger scallops. The fresher the scallops, the better, since they will release less liquid when cooked and will be moister when eaten. When you purchase scallops, always make sure they have a fresh smell (not of ammonia), are nice and firm, and are not floating in any milky liquid. The acidity of the rhubarb purée in this recipe acts like a squeeze of lemon in balancing the flavors of the scallops. I enjoy this seafood dish with light- to medium-bodied dry white wines with good acidity, such as a Chenin Blanc, Gewürztraminer, or dry Riesling. I also love a medium-bodied, very fruit-forward Pinot Noir, which balances nicely with the sweet-sour flavors in the rhubarb purée. GW

Rhubarb Purée
2 cups diced young rhubarb stalks (about ¾ pound)
½ tablespoon unsalted butter
½ cup Pinot Noir or dry red wine
1½ tablespoons honey
2 tablespoons sugar
Kosher salt and freshly ground black pepper

1 pound bay scallops
Kosher salt and freshly ground black pepper
1 teaspoon olive oil
1 tablespoon minced fresh chives or lemon thyme, for garnish
1 teaspoon finely grated lemon zest, for garnish

To prepare the purée, combine the rhubarb, butter, wine, and honey in a saucepan over medium heat. Cover and simmer for 5 to 7 minutes, until the rhubarb is soft when pierced with a knife. Stir in the sugar and cook for about 2 minutes, until the sugar is dissolved. Carefully pour the rhubarb mixture into a blender and purée until smooth. Season with salt and pepper. Return the purée to the saucepan and keep warm.

To prepare the scallops, remove the tough muscle from the side of each, if necessary. Rinse, pat them dry, and sprinkle with salt and pepper. Heat a large sauté pan over high heat and add the olive oil. When the oil is hot, add the scallops and sauté, tossing occasionally, for 3 to 4 minutes, until golden on all sides. The scallops should be opaque but still moist looking in the center (cut to test). Depending on the size of your sauté pan, you may have to sauté the scallops in two batches, adding another ½ teaspoon oil if needed.

To serve, spread 3 to 4 tablespoons of the rhubarb purée in a thin pool in the center of each plate. Divide the scallops evenly among the plates, placing them on top of the purée. Garnish with the minced chives and a pinch of lemon zest and serve immediately.

BIG BITES

61

Grilled Swordfish on Summer Garden Medley with Aioli

5 tablespoons olive oil

1 tablespoon drained capers

2 teaspoons freshly squeezed lemon juice

½ cup Chardonnay

1½ tablespoons sherry vinegar

2 tablespoons minced shallots

1 teaspoon minced serrano chile, seeded

Kosher salt and freshly ground black pepper

4 ears white corn

2 tablespoons unsalted butter, at room temperature

4 to 5 assorted heirloom tomatoes, seeded and cut into ¼-inch dice

1 cup Sweet 100 or other cherry tomatoes

1 cup diced green bell pepper

½ teaspoon minced fresh oregano

4 (6-ounce) swordfish steaks

½ to ¾ cup aioli (page 110)

Most of the cooking in this recipe is done outdoors on the barbecue—perfect for those hot summer days when you don't want to heat up your kitchen. The smoky, barbecue-roasted corn and sweet heirloom tomatoes in the vegetable medley blend nicely with the flavor of the grilled swordfish, creating a perfect backdrop for a medium-bodied Chardonnay. There are many styles of Chardonnay, so it's important to know if the wine is crisp, rich, and fruit-forward or oakey. The oakier Chardonnays tend to be fuller bodied with a higher alcohol content, which for my taste would be too much for this dish.   GW

Prepare a hot fire in a charcoal grill or preheat a gas grill to high.

Heat a small sauté pan over medium-high heat and add 2 tablespoons of the olive oil. When the oil is hot, add the capers and fry until crispy, 1 to 2 minutes. Transfer to paper towels to drain.

In a small bowl, prepare a vinaigrette by whisking together the lemon juice, wine, the remaining 3 tablespoons olive oil, and sherry vinegar. Add the shallots and chile and season with salt and pepper.

Place each ear of corn on a 12-inch piece of aluminum foil. Divide the butter among the ears and spread out to coat evenly. Lightly season each with salt and pepper. Wrap the foil securely around the corn, folding the ends so none of the butter will leak out. Place on the grill rack for 12 to 15 minutes, turning every 3 to 4 minutes so the corn is evenly roasted on all sides. Remove from the grill, open the foil, and allow to cool. When cool enough to handle, cut the kernels from the cobs and place in a bowl. Add all the tomatoes, the bell pepper, and oregano. Pour the vinaigrette over and toss to coat evenly.

After making sure the grill is still hot, brush the swordfish with a thin layer of olive oil on both sides. Salt and pepper lightly. Place on the grill rack and grill, turning once, for 3½ minutes on the first side and 3 minutes on the second side for medium rare, or until golden brown. If you prefer your fish cooked more, grill a bit longer.

To serve, divide the vegetable medley among 4 plates. Top each with a swordfish steak and spoon 2 to 3 tablespoons of aioli on each piece of fish. Garnish with the fried capers and serve immediately.

Rosemary and Garlic–Crusted Chicken Breasts with Port-Marinated Nectarines

Serves 6

We are lucky to have rosemary as a ground cover in our garden year-round, so I seem to always find uses for it, particularly when grilling. In this dish, I use the crisp garlic-rosemary crust and smoky flavor of the chicken to contrast with the dark, sweet glaze on the tender nectarines. You can substitute peaches for the nectarines; when selecting the fruit, make sure it is ripe but not soft. Leave the skin on, because the fruit will hold together better when grilling. I serve wild rice with this dish since its texture and flavor contrast well with the grilled nectarines. An off-dry Riesling will balance the sweetness found in the grilled fruit. I also enjoy a red wine such as a Sangiovese with lots of ripe berry flavors. GW

2 tablespoons port

¼ cup dark molasses

2 tablespoons sherry vinegar

½ cup honey

4 to 5 large nectarines, quartered

5 tablespoons finely chopped fresh rosemary

2 tablespoons minced garlic

1 tablespoon freshly squeezed lemon juice

1 tablespoon olive oil

½ teaspoon kosher salt

¼ teaspoon freshly ground black pepper

6 boneless, skinless chicken breast halves

Prepare a hot fire in a charcoal grill or preheat a gas grill to high.

In a bowl, stir together the port, molasses, vinegar, and honey. Add the nectarines and toss lightly to coat evenly. Marinate at room temperature for about 20 minutes.

In a small bowl, combine the rosemary, garlic, lemon juice, olive oil, salt, and pepper and mix well. Place the chicken breasts on a platter and coat each one with the rosemary-garlic mixture, pressing gently onto both sides to create a crust. Refrigerate for about 15 minutes.

When the grill is hot, remove the nectarines from the marinade, reserving the marinade. Place the nectarines on the grill rack and grill, turning once, until cooked through and tender but not mushy, about 8 minutes on each side. Grill the chicken breasts for about 10 minutes on the first side, then turn and grill the second side for 7 minutes, or until the meat is springy to the touch.

While the nectarines and chicken are grilling, pour the nectarine marinade into a small saucepan over medium-high heat and bring to a boil. Decrease the heat and simmer for about 10 minutes, until slightly thickened.

To serve, place a chicken breast on each plate. Drizzle the reduced marinade over the chicken and place 3 to 4 nectarine slices alongside. Serve immediately.

Wild Mushroom and Duck Pappardelle with Arugula

Serves 4

2 tablespoons olive oil

1 yellow onion, thinly sliced lengthwise

1 pound fresh wild mushrooms, such as chanterelle, hedgehog, or black trumpet, cleaned and thinly sliced

Kosher salt and freshly ground black pepper

4 cloves garlic, minced

2 cups chicken stock (page 111)

1 cup heavy cream

1 tablespoon fresh tarragon leaves

4 (6- to 8-ounce) duck breasts

¾ pound fresh or dried pappardelle

¼ pound arugula

I love cooking duck and this pasta dish always receives rave reviews from friends and family. This technique for cooking the breast is especially good for providing a crisp skin with an even pink color throughout the meat. The crispiness of the skin combined with the richness of both skin and meat is a fine contrast for the texture and flavor of the sharp arugula and earthy mushrooms. The key to this dish is waiting until the end to cook the pasta. The duck and sauce can always sit for a little bit, but when the pasta is ready, it must be served immediately. You can use portobello mushrooms or two to three ounces of dried, rehydrated wild mushrooms instead of the fresh ones. I always like Pinot Noir with duck, but a Merlot or Syrah would be equally delicious. KJ

Heat a heavy-bottomed, nonreactive pan over high heat and add the olive oil. Decrease the heat to medium, add the onion, and sauté, stirring often, until light golden brown, about 5 minutes. Increase the heat to high, add the mushrooms, and season with salt and pepper. Sauté, stirring often, until light golden brown, 3 to 5 minutes. Add the garlic and stir for 1 minute. Add the stock and scrape the toasted bits from the bottom of the pan. Bring to a simmer and cook for 10 minutes. Add the cream and tarragon, decrease the heat to medium, and cook at a low simmer for 10 minutes, or until slightly thickened. The sauce should coat the back of a spoon. Cover and keep warm.

Preheat the oven to 450°F and bring a large pot of salted water to a boil over high heat.

Trim the duck breasts of any excess fat and score the skin in a cross-hatch pattern. Do not cut all the way through to the meat. Heat an oven-proof sauté pan over medium-high heat. Season the duck with salt and pepper and place it, skin side down, in the hot pan. Cook until the skin is a light golden brown, about 5 minutes. Pour out the duck fat as it collects in the bottom of the pan. Place the pan in the oven with the duck still skin side down, and cook for another 5 to 7 minutes, until the meat side has just lost its raw color. Remove from the oven and turn over. Let rest in the pan in a warm place.

(continued)

Add the pappardelle to the boiling water and cook until al dente, 2 to 3 minutes for fresh pasta, 5 to 7 minutes for dried. While it is cooking, thinly slice the duck. Add any duck juices in the sauté pan or from slicing to the mushroom mixture and stir well. Drain the pasta and immediately toss gently with the mushroom mixture and the arugula until the pasta is thoroughly coated and the arugula wilts. Season with salt and pepper.

To assemble, divide the pasta among 4 plates and top with the sliced duck. Serve immediately.

Chicken Saltimbocca

Serves 4

2 tablespoons minced fresh rosemary

1 tablespoon minced fresh sage

1 tablespoon minced garlic

4 boneless, skinless chicken breast halves

4 to 6 slices prosciutto

¼ cup unsalted butter

Kosher salt and freshly ground black pepper

1 cup dry white wine, such as Chardonnay or Sauvignon Blanc

2 tablespoons freshly squeezed lemon juice

This savory dish was inspired by the classic Italian saltimbocca. Instead of veal, I use chicken breasts and add a bit of garlic. Pair with a rich, full-bodied Pinot Blanc or Chardonnay or, if you are a red wine fan, try a Sangiovese or Barbera. CW

In a small bowl, combine the rosemary, sage, and garlic.

Lay the chicken breasts flat on a work surface. Completely cover each piece of chicken with prosciutto. Divide the herb mixture among the breasts, spreading it out on top of the prosciutto. Starting at one short end of a chicken breast, roll it up evenly. Wrap a 10- to 12-inch length of kitchen twine around the center and tie snugly. Wrap a second piece of twine lengthwise around the ends of the roll, perpendicular to the first piece, and tie securely. Cut off the excess twine and discard. Repeat the rolling and tying with the remaining chicken breasts.

Heat a large sauté pan over medium-high heat and add the butter. When the butter is melted, place the chicken in the pan and brown evenly on all sides, about 5 minutes total. Season the chicken with salt and pepper. Add the wine and lemon juice, cover, and decrease the heat to medium-low. Simmer for about 30 minutes, until the meat is no longer pink. Place the chicken on a serving platter and remove the kitchen twine. Pour the juices from the pan over the breasts and serve at once.

Wild Mushroom–Stuffed Turkey Breast Grilled under a Brick

Serves 8

This is a fabulous way to cook turkey and keep it moist and succulent. The key is indirect heat, which I create in a kettle-style barbecue by making a fire toward one side of the grill. If you have a gas grill, turn the heat off on one half. By weighing it down, the turkey breast cooks very evenly with a crispy skin. It's wonderful at Thanksgiving or Christmas, but equally great year-round. My favorite wines with turkey are Riesling and Pinot Noir. By serving both an off-dry white wine and a versatile, medium-bodied red wine, you can please everyone. KJ

1 tablespoon olive oil

½ pound fresh wild mushrooms, such as chanterelle or hedgehog (you could substitute portobello), cut into bite-sized pieces

2 tablespoons minced shallots

1 tablespoon cognac or brandy

¼ cup heavy cream

Kosher salt and freshly ground black pepper

2 tablespoons chopped fresh sage

1 (4- to 5-pound) whole boneless turkey breast

2 bricks double-wrapped in aluminum foil

Heat a sauté pan over high heat and add the olive oil. When the oil is almost smoking, add the mushrooms and cook, stirring occasionally, until lightly golden, 7 to 8 minutes. Add the shallots and cook, stirring constantly, for 1 minute. Move the pan away from the burner and add the cognac. Taking care, tip the pan away from you and into the fire to ignite the cognac. (If you don't have a gas range, light with a match.) Return to the burner to cook until the flames die out. Add the cream and season with salt and pepper. Cook until most of the cream is absorbed, 2 to 3 minutes. Remove from the heat, add the sage, and toss gently.

Prepare a medium-hot fire toward one side of a charcoal grill or preheat half of a gas grill to medium-high. Separate the 2 halves of the turkey breast. Cover with plastic wrap and pound lightly with a meat mallet, cleaver, or pan to make the meat an even thickness. Lift up the fillet (the piece of meat that is loosely attached to the breast), keeping it attached. With a sharp knife, cut a pocket 1½ inches deep under the fillet. Repeat on the other half breast. Stuff the pockets with the mushroom mixture, folding the fillet over. Season both sides of the breasts with salt and pepper.

Place the breasts, skin side down, on the grill rack over the hot part of the fire. Top with the bricks and cover the barbecue. Cook until the skin turns golden brown, about 10 minutes. Move the breasts over indirect heat, turn them over, and replace the bricks. Re-cover the grill and open the vents near the turkey. Cook until the internal temperature registers 145°F on an instant-read thermometer, 40 to 50 minutes. Remove from the grill and let rest for 10 minutes.

Slice the breasts crosswise so that the stuffing shows in the center of each slice. Arrange on a platter and serve immediately.

Roasted Chicken with Apples and Onions, Fingerling Potatoes, and Wild Mushroom Sauce

1 (3½- to 4-pound) chicken

Kosher salt and freshly ground black pepper

1 large Gravenstein, Fuji, or Granny Smith apple, thickly sliced

1 large yellow onion, sliced

1 pound fingerling potatoes (you could substitute red, new, or Yukon gold)

6 tablespoons extra virgin olive oil

4 cups chicken stock (page 111)

½ pound fresh wild mushrooms, such as chanterelle or porcini (you could substitute portobello), quartered

½ cup dry white wine

1 tablespoon apple cider vinegar

1 teaspoon Dijon mustard

1 teaspoon finely minced shallots

1 pound mixed baby greens

This is the only way I have found to roast chicken in which the leg-thigh portion and the breast finish cooking at about the same time. You can also use this method of removing the backbone and laying the chicken out flat when grilling or smoking. The meat really retains its juices. Everything works together in this dish; the high oven temperature makes the skin very crispy, and the apples and onions become very sweet and saucy from steaming under the roasting chicken. This is a great crossover wine dish since it pairs well with both red and white varietals. I prefer it with stronger oak-aged whites, such as Chardonnay, and milder reds, such as Pinot Noir or Beaujolais. KJ

Preheat the oven to 450°F.

When flattening chicken, the object is to remove the backbone, cut through the rib cage, and keep it all in one piece, connected by the skin. To do this, lay the chicken breast-side down. Using a sharp knife, cut along the backbone, detaching the thigh bone from the backbone. Continue cutting along the backbone, through the rib cage, to the wing. Detach the wing joint from the back. Repeat on the other side and remove the backbone. Make a small incision at the bottom of either side of the breastbone. Crack the breastbone at the incisions. The chicken should lay fairly flat now. Season both sides with salt and pepper.

Place the apple and onion in a roasting pan just large enough to hold the chicken. Place the chicken, skin side up, on top of the apple and onion. Roast until the juices run clear when the chicken thigh is pierced with a knife, 50 to 60 minutes.

Begin preparing the potatoes halfway through the chicken roasting time. Place the potatoes in a small stockpot over high heat and add cold water to cover. Bring to a boil. Decrease the heat to achieve a simmer and cook until the potatoes are very tender when pierced with a knife, about 25 minutes. Drain and toss with 2 tablespoons of the olive oil and season with salt and pepper. It's fine if the potatoes get slightly mashed.

Bring the stock to a boil in a wide-rimmed saucepan over high heat. Decrease the heat to low and simmer until reduced by half, 12 to 15 minutes.

Heat a sauté pan over high heat and add 1 tablespoon of the olive oil. When the oil is almost smoking, add the mushrooms and sauté until golden brown, 3 to 5 minutes. Add the wine and scrape the toasted bits off the bottom of the pan. Stir in the reduced stock.

In a bowl, whisk together the cider vinegar, mustard, and the remaining 3 tablespoons olive oil. Add the shallots and season with salt and pepper. Add the greens and toss gently to coat.

Before serving, reheat the mushroom sauce over medium heat if necessary. To serve, cut the chicken into quarters. Place a breast or leg-thigh on each plate. Divide the potatoes and greens among the plates. With a slotted spoon, scoop the apples and onions from the roasting pan and place over the chicken. Drizzle the mushroom sauce over the chicken and serve immediately.

Roasted Cornish Game Hen with Cornbread, Sausage, and Dried Fruit Stuffing

Serves 6

Game hens are a pleasant alternative to chicken and just as simple to prepare. To make preparation even easier, I don't stuff the hens; I just spread the stuffing in the roasting pan and lay the birds on top. The juices from the game hens flow onto the stuffing, adding their flavor to the fruity mixture. For the stuffing, I use a packaged cornbread mix and make it first. While the cornbread is baking, I chop and prepare all of the other ingredients, including the hens. I prefer to use sourdough bread for the seasoned bread crumbs because it has a sharper, crisper flavor, but you could substitute other types of bread. Pinot Noir, with its medium body and full fruit, is one of my favorites wines to serve with this dish, but you might also try a Riesling if you prefer a white wine. The crisp acidity of the Riesling and its characteristic peach, apricot, and citrus flavors are particularly agreeable with this fruit stuffing. GW

Preheat the oven to 450°F.

To prepare the stuffing, in a sauté pan over medium heat, sauté the sausage for 6 to 8 minutes, until light brown. Drain the rendered fat from the pan into a small bowl and set aside. Place the sausage in a large bowl. Melt the butter in the same sauté pan over medium heat, add the onions and celery and sauté until tender, about 5 minutes. Add the onions, celery, cornbread, apricots, cranberries, and bread crumbs to the sausage and mix well. Stir in the eggs, melted butter, and sage and season with salt and pepper. Taste the stuffing and if you think it needs more flavor, add some of the rendered fat. Fold in enough chicken stock to provide some moisture. Don't add too much since it will make the stuffing soggy; the stuffing should not stick together when you squeeze a handful.

Cut the game hens in half lengthwise. Rub them with olive oil and season with salt and pepper. Grease a 9 by 13-inch baking dish, fill the bottom with the stuffing, and snugly pack the hens on top, cut side down. Roast for 20 minutes. Decrease the heat to 375°F and continue to roast for about another 25 minutes, or until the juices run clear when a thigh is pierced with a knife.

To serve, place a spoonful of stuffing on each plate, top with half a game hen, and serve immediately.

Stuffing

1 pound pork sausage, crumbled

2 tablespoons unsalted butter

2 cups chopped yellow onion (about 2 onions)

2 cups chopped celery (about 8 stalks)

6 cups coarsely crumbled yellow cornbread

1 cup chopped dried apricots

1 cup dried cranberries

1 cup seasoned sourdough bread crumbs (page 110)

2 eggs, slightly beaten

½ cup unsalted butter, melted

2 teaspoons minced fresh sage, or 1 tablespoon dried sage

Kosher salt and freshly ground black pepper

1 cup chicken stock, or as needed (page 111)

3 Cornish game hens

1 tablespoon olive oil

Kosher salt and freshly ground black pepper

Meatloaf with Shiitake Mashed Potatoes

1 tablespoon olive oil

2 yellow onions, minced

10 cloves garlic, minced

½ cup fine sourdough bread crumbs
(page 110)

1 pound ground beef

1 pound ground pork or fresh
sausage meat

2 eggs, beaten

2 tablespoons minced oil-packed
sun-dried tomatoes, drained

1 tablespoon diced jalapeño
chile, seeded

1 tablespoon Worcestershire sauce

⅓ cup tomato paste

2 teaspoons kosher salt

1 teaspoon freshly ground
black pepper

1 teaspoon paprika

2 pounds Yellow Finn or Yukon gold
potatoes, peeled and quartered

½ cup unsalted butter

¾ cup heavy cream

1½ cups fresh shiitake mushrooms,
stemmed and thinly sliced

We often overlook recipes that we grew up with, forgetting fond memories of such classics as meatloaf and mashed potatoes. I prefer the texture of "home-style" mashed potatoes, so I use a hand potato masher, which leaves the mixture somewhat lumpy. The trick to a good meatloaf is to keep it moist, so it holds together when slicing. Hot or cold, meatloaf is often better the second day. Serve with a balanced, medium-bodied red wine, such as a Syrah, Merlot, or Zinfandel. GW

Preheat the oven to 350°F. Heat a sauté pan over medium-high heat and add the olive oil. When the oil is hot, add the onions and 6 of the garlic cloves and cook until the onions are lightly golden and translucent, 5 to 8 minutes. Transfer to a large bowl and add the bread crumbs, beef, pork, eggs, tomatoes, jalapeño, Worcestershire, tomato paste, 1 teaspoon of the salt, the pepper, and paprika. Mix thoroughly and then transfer to a 9 by 4½ by 2½-inch loaf pan. Press down to shape the top and then cover with aluminum foil. Bake for about 45 minutes, until lightly browned and crispy on top. Remove the foil and continue cooking for 30 minutes, until a brown crust forms on top. Remove from the oven and let stand for 10 minutes before serving.

While the meatloaf is cooking, place the potatoes in a saucepan over high heat and add the remaining 1 teaspoon salt and water to cover. Cover and bring to a boil. Cook for 15 to 20 minutes, until tender when pierced with a fork. Do not undercook as they will not mash as smoothly. Drain the potatoes and return them to the saucepan. Add 4 tablespoons of the butter and mash with a potato masher until lumpy.

In a small saucepan over low heat, combine the remaining 4 tablespoons butter and the remaining 4 cloves garlic. Stir frequently. Cook for 6 minutes, or until very tender. Add the mushrooms and cook, stirring frequently, until the liquid has evaporated and they are beginning to brown, 4 to 6 minutes. Add the cream and simmer for 5 minutes, until heated through but not boiling. Add to the mashed potatoes and stir well. Season with salt and pepper.

To serve, reheat the potatoes if necessary, adding a bit more butter or cream if needed to prevent sticking. Cut the meatloaf in the pan into 1-inch-thick slices. Place a scoop of potatoes and a slice of meatloaf on each plate and serve immediately.

Balsamic-Mushroom Burgers with Caramelized Red Wine Onions

Serves 6

Whenever I use mushrooms as a burger topping, they always seem to slide off. By combining the mushrooms with the meat you eliminate that problem. I also like mixing the salt and pepper into the meat so it gets seasoned all the way through, not just on the outside. Sometimes I add dry-cured olives and truffle oil to the beef for even more flavor interest. These burgers are great with just about any red wine. KJ

Fill a large bowl with ice.

Heat a large sauté pan over high heat and add 1 tablespoon of the olive oil. When the oil is hot, add the mushrooms. Cook, stirring often, until the mushrooms are cooked through and light golden brown, 3 to 5 minutes. Decrease the heat to low, add the garlic and vinegar, stir well, and season with salt and pepper. Transfer the mushrooms to a bowl and place in the bowl of ice to cool. When cool, remove from the ice bowl and add the ground beef. Season with salt and pepper and mix well.

Heat a large sauté pan over high heat and add the remaining 1 tablespoon olive oil. When the oil is hot, add the onions and season with salt and pepper. Cook, stirring often, until the onions begin to brown and caramelize, about 10 minutes. Add the wine and decrease the heat to medium. Cook, stirring occasionally, until the liquid evaporates, about 5 minutes. Add the water and cook until evaporated, another 5 minutes. The onions should be soft and caramelized.

Form the meat mixture into 6 patties about 4½ inches wide by ¾ inch thick. Preheat the broiler. Heat 2 large sauté pans over high heat. Add the burgers, decrease the heat to medium, and cover. Cook for 3 to 4 minutes, until the underside is browned. Remove the covers, turn the burgers over, and cook the second side, uncovered, for 3 to 4 minutes, until browned. The burgers will be medium rare and still feel a little soft when you press the middle with your finger. Lightly toast the buns under the broiler while the burgers are cooking.

To serve, place each burger on a bun bottom, top with the onions, cover with a bun top, and serve immediately.

2 tablespoons olive oil

1½ pounds fresh portobello mushrooms, stemmed and cut into ¼-inch dice (about 3 cups)

1 tablespoon minced garlic

1 tablespoon balsamic vinegar

Kosher salt and freshly ground black pepper

2 pounds ground beef

2 yellow onions, thinly sliced (about 2 cups)

¼ cup red wine

½ cup water

6 large burger buns

Grilled Flank Steak on Corn Fritters with Sweet 100 Salsa

Marinade

2 cups dry red wine

⅓ cup balsamic vinegar

3 tablespoons raspberry vinegar

2 tablespoons Worcestershire sauce

1 bay leaf

½ teaspoon kosher salt

½ teaspoon freshly ground
 black pepper

2 pounds beef flank steak

Salsa

2 cups Sweet 100 or other cherry
 tomatoes, quartered

3 tablespoons minced shallots

2 tablespoons minced fresh chives

3 tablespoons chopped fresh basil

2 teaspoons minced garlic

1 teaspoon chopped jalapeño
 chile, seeded

3 tablespoons freshly squeezed
 lime juice

5 teaspoons pure maple syrup

½ teaspoon kosher salt

½ teaspoon freshly ground
 black pepper

Corn Fritters

2 eggs

¾ cup buttermilk

⅔ cup yellow cornmeal

2 tablespoons all-purpose flour

½ teaspoon kosher salt

2½ cups corn kernels (about 5 ears)

2 tablespoons vegetable oil

Flank steak has a sinewy texture that becomes more tender when marinated. The easy marinade included here can be prepared a day ahead so all you have to do the next evening is take the marinated steak out of the refrigerator and grill it. The salsa can be prepared several hours ahead of time; if you can't find Sweet 100 tomatoes, substitute your favorite ripe cherry tomato. Silver Queen corn or a white corn variety adds a nice color variation to the corn fritters, but yellow corn can be used just as easily. I make larger fritters because I like their appearance under the steak, but you could make smaller ones if you prefer. Open a bottle of Merlot or Zinfandel with this dish, as the fruit flavors and soft tannins will work well with the steak and tomato salsa. GW

To prepare the marinade, whisk together the wine, vinegars, Worcestershire sauce, bay leaf, salt, and pepper in a small bowl. Pour into a resealable plastic bag, add the steak, seal, and turn to coat evenly. Place in a pan with sides (in case it leaks) and refrigerate for at least 2 hours or up to overnight. Turn several times to coat evenly.

To prepare the salsa, combine the tomatoes, shallots, chives, basil, garlic, jalapeño, lime juice, and maple syrup in a bowl and stir well. Season with salt and pepper. Set aside for at least 30 minutes or up to 4 hours to allow the flavors to marry.

Prepare a medium fire in a charcoal grill or preheat a gas grill to medium.

To prepare the fritters, preheat the oven to 250°F. In a bowl, whisk together the eggs and buttermilk. Add the cornmeal, flour, and salt and stir until smooth. Add the corn and stir until well coated. Heat a large sauté pan over medium-high heat and add 1 tablespoon of the oil. When the oil is hot but not smoking, drop about ¼ cup of the batter into the pan to make a fritter 4 to 6 inches in diameter. Cook, turning once, until lightly browned, about 3 minutes on each side. Place on a platter, cover with aluminum foil, and keep warm in the oven. Repeat with the remaining batter, adding oil to the pan as necessary to prevent sticking. Depending on the size, you should have 4 to 6 fritters.

Remove the flank steak from the marinade, discarding the marinade. Place the steak on the grill rack and cook, turning once, for 3 to 4 minutes on each side for rare or until the internal temperature registers

125°F on an instant-read thermometer. Watch carefully while grilling as flank steaks cook quickly and can become tough when overdone. When done, transfer the steak to a cutting board, cover with foil, and let rest for 10 minutes.

To serve, thinly slice the steak on an angle against the grain. Place a fritter on each plate and overlap halfway with 4 to 5 slices of steak. Spoon salsa over the top and serve immediately.

Thyme-Barbecued New York Steak with Corn and Blue Cheese Pudding

Serves 4

When I put meals together, there are certain combinations that I like to experiment with. Combining sweet flavors with acidity and salt is one of these. In this pudding, the juxtaposition of sweet corn and salty, acidic blue cheese holds its own against the hearty barbecued steak. The easiest way to cut the corn off the cob is to place it root side down in a mixing bowl. Hold the tip of the cob with one hand and cut the kernels off into the bowl. This well-balanced meat dish is wonderful with hearty red wines such as Zinfandel, Petite Sirah, and Cabernet as well as white wines that are of equal weight and body. Accompany this dish with a lightly dressed green salad. KJ

1 cup puréed corn kernels (about 4 ears)

½ cup corn kernels (about 1 ear)

3 eggs

⅓ cup milk

½ cup sour cream

1 jalapeño chile, seeds removed, finely minced

¼ cup crumbled mild blue cheese, such as Maytag Blue

Kosher salt and freshly ground black pepper

2 (12-ounce) New York steaks, about 1½ inches thick

1 tablespoon chopped fresh thyme, stems reserved

Prepare a small fire in a charcoal grill or preheat a gas grill to medium-low. Preheat the oven to 350°F.

Lightly butter a 2-quart baking dish. In a bowl, combine the puréed corn, corn kernels, eggs, milk, sour cream, jalapeño, and cheese and mix thoroughly. Season with salt and pepper. Pour into the prepared baking dish and bake for about 1 hour, until the top is golden brown and the pudding is set throughout.

Season the steaks with salt and pepper and press the thyme onto both sides. Add the thyme stems to the fire. Place the steaks on the grill rack and cover. Cook, turning every 5 minutes, until the internal temperature registers 120°F on an instant-read thermometer, about 15 minutes for rare. Transfer to a plate and lightly cover with aluminum foil. Let rest for 10 minutes.

To serve, slice the meat on the diagonal against the grain. Arrange one-fourth of the slices on each plate, and place a spoonful of the pudding alongside. Serve immediately.

Tri-Tip Steak with Smashed Potatoes, Carrots, and Corn, and Red Wine–Tarragon Butter Sauce

Serves 4

1½ to 2 pounds beef tri-tip steak

Kosher salt and freshly ground black pepper

1 tablespoon olive oil

1 cup dry red wine

¼ cup unsalted butter

2 sprigs tarragon

1½ pounds Yukon gold or white potatoes, quartered (4 to 5 potatoes)

½ pound carrots, peeled (about 2 carrots)

½ cup extra virgin olive oil

1 teaspoon freshly squeezed lemon juice

1 cup fresh corn kernels (about 2 ears)

Tri-tip steak is one of my favorites in terms of tenderness and flavor. The cut comes from the area of the loin where the strip loin, fillet, and top sirloin all converge. It is great cooked on the barbecue as well as roasted, as in this dish. Here, I collect all of the nice juices from the roasting pan and use them in the wine sauce. Using red wine for the sauce adds a little acidity to the dish, which is especially good in balancing the richness of the potatoes, carrots, and corn. I really like most red wines with steak, but Merlot and Pinot Noir are particularly good with this preparation. *KJ*

Preheat the oven to 375°F. Season the tri-tip with salt and pepper. Heat an ovenproof sauté pan over high heat and add the olive oil. When the oil is hot, add the steak and cook until the underside is nicely browned, about 5 minutes. Turn over and place in the oven. Cook until the internal temperature registers 120°F on an instant-read thermometer, 15 to 20 minutes for medium rare. Remove from the oven, transfer to a plate, loosely cover with aluminum foil, and let rest for 10 minutes.

Add the wine to the pan and scrape the brown bits off the bottom of the pan. Place over medium heat and simmer for about 10 minutes, until reduced to about ½ cup. Increase the heat to high, add the butter and tarragon, and cook for another 2 minutes, until slightly thickened. Season with salt and pepper and keep warm.

Meanwhile, in a small stockpot over high heat, combine the potatoes and carrots, add water to cover, and bring to a boil. Decrease the heat to achieve a simmer and cook until the potatoes are very easily pierced with a knife, about 20 minutes. Drain and return to the pot. Add the extra virgin olive oil and lemon juice. With a wooden spoon, smash everything together until still a trifle lumpy. Stir in the corn and season with salt and pepper.

Pour any juices that have collected from the meat into the sauce and stir well. Slice the tri-tip thinly on an angle against the grain. Arrange one-fourth of the steak slices on each plate, and place a scoop of the smashed potatoes alongside. Drizzle a couple spoonfuls of the sauce over the steak and serve immediately.

Rosemary-Roasted Pork Loin with Carrot-Fennel Purée and Swiss Chard

6 cloves garlic, minced

3 tablespoons chopped fresh rosemary

1 teaspoon kosher salt

1 teaspoon freshly ground black pepper

3 tablespoons olive oil

3 pounds boneless pork loin

1½ cups dry white wine

Carrot-Fennel Purée

1 tablespoon unsalted butter

2 carrots, peeled and sliced

2 cloves garlic, chopped

1 fennel bulb, coarsely chopped

1 leek, white part only, sliced

1¼ cups chicken stock, more as needed (page 111)

1 teaspoon balsamic vinegar

½ teaspoon honey

Greens

1 bunch Swiss chard, stemmed and coarsely chopped

1 teaspoon kosher salt

1 tablespoon unsalted butter

½ teaspoon freshly squeezed lemon juice

Freshly ground black pepper

Along with flavor, I also consider texture and visual presentation when putting together a meal. For example, this combination of pork loin with chewy, green chard and a velvety carrot purée creates a nice balance of textures as well as a pleasing appearance. Pork loins are often sold in two-piece packages, wrapped in netting. For roasting more quickly and evenly, separate the pieces. Try a relatively rich, medium-bodied Chardonnay with this pork loin. The body and richness of many Chardonnays are good matches for similarly weighted foods. Other types of wine that may show similar pairing characteristics include Pinot Blanc, Viognier, or rich, barrel-fermented styles of Sauvignon Blanc. GW

Preheat the oven to 400°F.

In a small bowl, combine the garlic, rosemary, salt, and pepper and mix well. Stir in the olive oil.

Place the pork loin on a rack in a roasting pan. With the tip of a sharp knife, make 1-inch slits into the top and sides of the pork. Coat on all sides with the rosemary mixture, pressing it into the slits. Place the pan on the center rack of the oven and bake for about 40 minutes, until the internal temperature registers 145°F on an instant-read thermometer. Remove from the oven, transfer to a cutting board, and loosely cover with aluminum foil. Let rest for 10 to 15 minutes before slicing.

Place the roasting pan over medium-high heat and add the wine, scraping up the toasted bits from the bottom and sides of the pan. Bring to a boil, stirring constantly. Decrease the heat and simmer for 10 minutes. Keep the sauce warm.

While the pork is roasting, prepare the purée. Heat a saucepan over medium-high heat and add the butter. When the butter is melted, add the carrots, garlic, fennel, and leek and sauté until the leek becomes translucent, about 5 minutes. Add the stock and bring to a boil. Cover and cook over low heat for about 15 minutes, until the carrots and fennel are tender. In batches if necessary, transfer the vegetables and stock to a blender or food processor and purée until smooth. Be careful with the hot liquids! Return to the saucepan and stir in the vinegar and honey. Keep warm over low heat, stirring often to prevent scorching.

To prepare the greens, place the chard in a sauté pan over high heat and pour in water to cover. Stir in the salt. Cover, bring to a boil, and cook until tender, 3 to 4 minutes. Drain in a colander. In the same pan over high heat, melt the butter. Whisk in the lemon juice. Add the chard and toss in the pan to heat through. Season with salt and pepper.

To serve, cut the pork into ½-inch slices. Divide the purée and greens among 4 plates. Place 2 to 3 slices of pork on each serving of purée and drizzle with the sauce. Serve immediately.

Pork Tenderloin with Spicy Pesto, Linguine, and Braised Greens

Serves 4

Pesto is the overriding flavor in this dish, embellishing the mild pork while taming the bitter greens. When making a pesto, I like to use regular olive oil to process the basil, and then add the extra virgin olive oil afterward by hand. The food processor tends to break down extra virgin olive oil, making it taste bitter. By adding it at the end, you retain its fruitiness and freshness. To complement this fruitiness, serve either a fruity red wine, such as a Syrah or Zinfandel, or a crisp, fruity white, such as a Riesling or Viognier. KG

Season the pork loin with salt and pepper. Set aside in the refrigerator while making the pesto.

To prepare the pesto, combine the basil and olive oil in a small food processor. Process until very finely ground. Transfer to a bowl and stir in the extra virgin olive oil, garlic, jalapeño, and Parmesan.

Heat a sauté pan over high heat. Add a little olive oil and then the pork loin. Sear the pork until browned on all sides, 5 to 7 minutes. Decrease the heat to medium, add the collard greens and tomatoes, cover, and cook for 7 to 10 minutes, until the internal temperature of the pork registers 145°F on an instant-read thermometer. Remove the pan from the heat, transfer the pork to a plate, and loosely cover with aluminum foil. Let rest for about 10 minutes before slicing.

Bring a large pot of salted water to a boil over high heat and add the pasta. Cook according to the package instructions, until al dente. Drain in a colander and return to the pot. Add the pesto and the collard greens mixture and toss gently. Season with salt and pepper.

To serve, divide the pasta among 4 plates. Slice the pork crosswise on an angle and divide among the plates. Serve immediately.

2 (8- to 10-ounce) pork tenderloins

Kosher salt and freshly ground black pepper

Pesto
1 cup packed fresh basil leaves

¼ cup olive oil

¼ cup extra virgin olive oil

3 cloves garlic, minced

2 jalapeño chiles, seeded and finely chopped

¼ cup finely grated Parmesan cheese

Olive oil, for sautéing

1 bunch collard greens, stemmed and torn into bite-sized pieces

1 pound tomatoes, peeled, seeded, and coarsely chopped

¾ pound dried linguine

Chile-Rubbed Pork Chops with Corn Spoonbread and Cilantro Salsa

Spoonbread
1²/₃ cups water

½ cup plus 2 tablespoons unsalted butter

1¼ cups yellow cornmeal

1 tablespoon sugar

1 cup buttermilk or heavy cream

Kosher salt and freshly ground black pepper

7 egg whites

Salsa
2 Anaheim chiles, cored and diced

1 jalapeño chile, cored and diced

2 tablespoons coarsely chopped cilantro

1 tablespoon minced garlic

1 teaspoon freshly squeezed lime juice, more as needed

Kosher salt and freshly ground black pepper

4 (12-ounce) bone-in pork chops, each 1 inch thick

1 tablespoon chile powder

1 tablespoon kosher salt

½ teaspoon ground cayenne pepper

Spoonbread is a lighter version of cornbread; the addition of whipped egg whites makes it almost like a soufflé. This lightness helps to balance the hearty pork and the spicy intensity of the chile rub and cilantro salsa. A little hot sauce or a pinch of cayenne pepper are good additions if you like a spicier salsa. Zinfandel or any fruity, powerful red wine served with this dish is a tasty bonus. KJ

To prepare the spoonbread, preheat the oven to 325°F and butter a shallow 2-quart baking dish.

In a large saucepan, bring the water and butter to a boil over high heat. Slowly add the cornmeal, stirring constantly. Cook until slightly thickened, 2 to 3 minutes. Remove from the heat, add the sugar and buttermilk, and stir until blended. Season with salt and pepper.

Place the egg whites in a clean, dry bowl. With an electric mixer on high speed or by hand, whip the whites until tripled in volume and soft peaks form. Carefully fold into the cornmeal mixture, a third at a time. Transfer the batter to the prepared baking dish. Place the dish inside a larger pan and place in the oven. Fill the outside pan with enough boiling water to come halfway up the sides of the spoonbread pan (see page 118 for tips on water baths). Bake until golden brown on top and just set, about 25 minutes. You can expect the spoonbread to fall after it is removed from the oven.

Prepare a medium fire in a charcoal grill or preheat a gas grill to medium.

To prepare the salsa, combine the chiles, cilantro, garlic, and lime juice in a small bowl. Taste and adjust the seasoning with salt, pepper, and additional lime juice, if necessary.

Trim any extra fat off the pork chops. In a small bowl, combine the chile powder, salt, and cayenne. Sprinkle the spices on both sides of the pork chops and thoroughly rub in. Place on the grill rack and grill, turning once, for 8 to 10 minutes on each side, until the internal temperature registers 145°F on an instant-read thermometer. Transfer to a platter and let rest for 5 minutes before serving.

To serve, place a portion of spoonbread on each plate. Lean a chop against the spoonbread and garnish with the salsa.

Pork Kebabs on Vineyard Skewers with Mission Figs and Grapes

Serves 4

I grill these kebabs on grapevine skewers, which contribute a wonderful smoky quality to the dish, but any skewer will do. Originally from South America, quinoa (pronounced KEEN-wah) is a very nutritious, high-protein grain that is lower in carbohydrates than most other grains. Look for it in natural food stores and some markets. If you can't find it, you can substitute an equal amount of brown or basmati rice. The rich, earthy flavors of fresh figs and the complex spices in the pork rub offer a perfect foil for the ripe cherry flavors of a Merlot. GW

To prepare the rub, in a small bowl, mix together the curry powder, paprika, cumin, coriander, cinnamon, and nutmeg. (The rub mixture may be made in advance and stored in an airtight container for up to 1 month.)

To prepare the marinade, in another small bowl, mix together the lemon juice, wine, olive oil, and garlic.

Assemble the kebabs on 8-inch skewers, alternating between the pork cubes, figs, and grapes. Rub well with the spice mixture. Place the kebabs in a flat pan and evenly pour the marinade over all. Marinate in the refrigerator for at least 1 hour or up to overnight, turning the skewers once or twice.

Prepare a hot fire in a charcoal grill or preheat a gas grill to high.

In a saucepan over high heat, combine the quinoa and water. Bring to a boil, decrease the heat to achieve a simmer, cover, and cook for 10 to 15 minutes, until all the water is absorbed and the grains are tender. Season with salt and pepper.

While the quinoa is cooking, season the kebabs with salt and pepper. Place on the grill rack and grill, turning once, for about 10 minutes, until the pork is cooked through but still moist.

To serve, stir the pine nuts and mint into the quinoa and divide among 4 plates. Place 2 to 3 kebabs on the quinoa. Sprinkle on salt to taste and squeeze a wedge of lemon over each serving. Garnish with lemon zest and serve immediately.

Rub
1 teaspoon curry powder

¼ teaspoon paprika

½ teaspoon ground cumin

¼ teaspoon ground coriander

⅛ teaspoon ground cinnamon

¼ teaspoon ground nutmeg

Marinade
3 tablespoons freshly squeezed Meyer lemon juice (or equal parts orange juice and lemon juice)

¼ cup Merlot

3 tablespoons olive oil

1 teaspoon chopped garlic

1½ pounds pork tenderloin, cut into 1-inch cubes

12 fresh Mission figs, ends trimmed, halved lengthwise

¼ pound large firm red Flame or Thompson seedless grapes

1 cup quinoa

2 cups water

Kosher salt and freshly ground black pepper

¾ cup pine nuts, toasted (page 118)

3 to 4 fresh mint leaves, cut into chiffonade

½ lemon, cut into quarters, for serving

1 teaspoon finely grated lemon zest, for garnish

Goat Cheese–Stuffed Veal Chop with Herb-Garlic Roasted Potatoes

Serves 4

A big, juicy veal chop is hard to pass up and when stuffed with goat cheese, it can put an elegant twist on casual dining. You can use plain goat cheese or one of the varieties of seasoned goat cheeses flavored with pepper or chives. The bread crumbs help hold the stuffing together. The potatoes can be made a day ahead and are great to take on picnics as a potato salad substitute. For this particular dish, I begin by preparing the potatoes, then the stuffing, and finally the veal. A big-bodied, rich Chardonnay will do nicely with the richness found in the cheese stuffing, but I also enjoy a medium-bodied Pinot Noir, Barbera, or lighter-styled Syrah.   CW

Preheat the oven to 400°F. Place a rack in the middle position.

In a roasting pan, combine the potatoes and garlic. Drizzle with the olive oil and toss to coat evenly. Add 2 tablespoons of the fresh herbs and toss well. Place in the oven and roast for about 45 minutes, until the potatoes are cooked through and golden brown. Halfway through the cooking time, turn with a spatula to roast evenly. Remove from the oven and sprinkle with the remaining 2 tablespoons fresh herbs. Season with salt and pepper. Maintain the oven temperature at 400°F.

To prepare the stuffing, mix together the bread crumbs, salt, pepper, paprika, oregano, tarragon, onion powder, and cayenne in a bowl. Add the goat cheese and work into the bread crumbs with your hands, until the bread crumbs are incorporated and the mixture holds together loosely.

On a cutting board, insert a sharp knife into the "tail" end of a veal chop and cut toward the T-bone on the loin side, making a small 2-inch pocket on one side of the chop. Repeat with the remaining chops. With your fingers, gently stuff the goat cheese mixture into the pocket of each chop, making a thin layer inside the meat. The stuffing should be divided evenly among the chops. Season both sides of the chops with salt and pepper.

Heat a large sauté pan over high heat and add the olive oil. When the oil is hot, add the chops and sear, turning once, for about 2 minutes on each side, until golden brown. Carefully remove from the sauté pan with a spatula so you do not lose the stuffing and place in a baking dish. Place in the oven and roast for about 12 minutes, until the chops are pink and juicy inside.

(continued)

Roasted Potatoes

12 small to medium new potatoes, cut into bite-sized pieces

20 cloves garlic (about 2 heads), peeled

2 tablespoons olive oil

¼ cup mixed chopped fresh herbs, such as thyme, mint, rosemary, sage, oregano, and tarragon

Kosher salt and freshly ground black pepper

Stuffing

½ cup fresh bread crumbs (page 110)

½ teaspoon salt

½ teaspoon freshly ground black pepper

1 teaspoon paprika

1 teaspoon ground oregano

1 teaspoon finely chopped fresh tarragon

1 teaspoon onion powder

½ teaspoon ground cayenne pepper

6 ounces fresh goat cheese (chèvre), crumbled

4 (10- to 12-ounce) veal loin chops, each 1½ inches thick

Kosher salt and freshly ground black pepper

2 teaspoons olive oil

½ cup port

1 cup veal or chicken stock (pages 116 and 111)

Place the sauté pan over high heat and add the port and stock, scraping the toasted bits from the bottom of the pan. Cook until the sauce thickens slightly, about 5 minutes. Season with salt and pepper.

To serve, place a chop in the center of each plate and surround with potatoes and garlic. Spoon some sauce over each chop. Serve immediately.

Cinnamon and Cumin–Crusted Lamb with Basil-Mint Aioli

Serves 4

Istanbul, Turkey, was my inspiration for this lamb dish. Big round baskets of cinnamon and cumin are everywhere in the markets, scenting the air with their lively aromas. Lamb seems to be the national dish of Turkey, so it was natural to combine these flavors. The cooking time for the lamb will depend greatly on what type of lamb you use. The more expensive domestic lamb, usually from California or Colorado, tends to be much larger in size than the more readily available New Zealand and Australian lamb. Ask your butcher for a few ounces of lamb scraps or some bones to enrich the sauce. The robust fruit flavors and tannins in Cabernet or Syrah pair well with the spicy flavors of this dish. KJ

½ cup aioli (page 110)

1 teaspoon minced fresh basil

1 teaspoon minced fresh mint

8 (6- to 8-ounce) lamb loin chops, 1½ inches thick

1 tablespoon ground cinnamon

1 tablespoon ground cumin

1 bunch fresh thyme

1 bunch fresh oregano

Kosher salt and freshly ground black pepper

Extra virgin olive oil

2 cups veal demi-glace (page 117)

1 cup dry red wine

1 tablespoon coarsely chopped fresh flat-leaf parsley, for garnish

In a bowl, combine the aioli, basil, and mint and stir well. Cover and refrigerate until needed.

Trim the lamb chops, leaving a thin layer of fat around the outside. Reserve any meat from the trimming. Heat a small sauté pan over medium heat. Add the cinnamon and cumin and toast for 2 to 3 minutes, stirring constantly, until very aromatic. Remove from the heat and spread on a plate to cool.

Pick the leaves off the thyme and oregano and reserve the stems. Coat both sides of the lamb, first with the cinnamon-cumin mixture and then with the oregano and thyme leaves. Season with salt and pepper. Drizzle both sides with olive oil. Refrigerate for at least 1 hour or up to 24 hours.

Preheat the oven to 350°F. Prepare a medium fire in a charcoal grill or preheat a gas grill to medium.

On a baking sheet, roast the reserved lamb scraps in the oven until light golden brown, 7 to 10 minutes. In a saucepan over high heat, combine the scraps with the demi-glace, wine, and reserved herb stems. Bring to a simmer, decrease the heat, and simmer for 30 minutes. Pass through a fine-meshed sieve, capturing the liquid. Return the liquid to the pan and keep warm over low heat.

Place the lamb on the grill rack and grill, turning once, for about 10 minutes on each side for medium rare, or until the internal temperature registers 120°F on an instant-read thermometer. Transfer to a cutting board and loosely cover with aluminum foil. Let rest for 5 minutes.

To serve, place 2 chops on each plate. Spoon a couple tablespoons of the sauce over the lamb and garnish with the aioli and parsley.

Grilled Lamb Burgers with Spiced Mayonnaise

Serves 6

Spiced Mayonnaise

½ cup mayonnaise

4 teaspoons freshly squeezed
    lemon juice

¼ teaspoon ground nutmeg

¼ teaspoon ground cloves

1 teaspoon ground cinnamon

2 pounds ground lamb

1 tablespoon chopped garlic

3 tablespoons finely chopped
    fresh mint

Kosher salt and freshly ground
    black pepper

6 hamburger buns

Favorite burger condiments, such as
    baby lettuces, sliced tomatoes, and
    sliced onions

Sometimes we overlook simple meals that can be created by just changing the cut or type of meat in an old standard. Here's an example of combining flavors associated with other lamb recipes (mint, garlic, and the spices of Middle Eastern cuisine) with an "All-American" burger. Adding spices to store-bought mayonnaise is a great shortcut to a tasty, spicy spread for the lamb burgers and tangy lemon juice further brightens the flavors. I have also served these burgers, minus the buns, with basmati rice seasoned with currants and the same spices that I add to the mayonnaise. Ground lamb can be found in your local grocery, but if you don't see it, you can ask your butcher to grind a lamb shoulder. The burgers are sublime when served with a robust Zinfandel that will match the burger's juicy tenderness or a minty Cabernet Sauvignon that will complement its flavors.   GW

Prepare a medium-hot fire in a charcoal grill or preheat a gas grill to medium-high.

In a small bowl, whisk together the mayonnaise and the lemon juice. Add the nutmeg, cloves, and cinnamon. Stir until well blended.

In a bowl, combine the ground lamb, garlic, and mint and season with salt and pepper. Mix with your hands until well blended. Form into 6 equal-sized patties, 3½ to 4 inches across and 1½ inches thick.

Place the lamb burgers on the grill rack, directly over the heat. Cook until medium-rare, 5 minutes on the first side, and about 4 more minutes on the second side. While the burgers are grilling, put the buns on the outside edges of the rack and toast until golden brown.

To serve, spread the spiced mayonnaise on the toasted buns. Place the burgers on the bun bottoms along with your favorite burger condiments, add the tops, and enjoy!

Lavender and Thyme–Scented Lamb with Flageolet Beans and Swiss Chard

1 teaspoon fresh lavender flowers

1 teaspoon fresh thyme leaves

¼ cup kosher salt

2 tablespoons olive oil

½ cup peeled and diced carrot

½ cup diced yellow onion

1 cup flageolet beans, soaked in
    4 cups water for at least 8 hours
    or overnight

About 4 cups chicken stock (page 111)

5 cloves garlic, halved

¼ cup dried cherries

4 (5-ounce) lamb loin chops, each
    1½ inches thick

1 bunch Swiss chard, ribs removed,
    leaves coarsely chopped

1 tablespoon chopped fresh flat-leaf
    parsley, for garnish

Lavender is a classic ingredient in herbes de Provence and is used in everything from soap to perfume to cooking in southern France. It grows quite well here in northern California as well, and the kitchen garden at the restaurant has always produced huge bushes. Putting the lavender in the seasoning salt really helps the flavor cling to the meat. You can make seasoned salt with any number of different flavorings, from garlic to hot chiles. Enjoy a robust Cabernet Sauvignon, Merlot, or Syrah with this rustic dish; their fruit flavors and full bodies complement the lamb and beans.

If you forget to soak the beans, you can do a "quick soak" by totally covering the beans with water and bringing them to a boil. Turn off the heat, let them sit for 30 minutes, drain, and cook according to the recipe instructions.   *KJ*

In a small bowl, combine the lavender, thyme, and salt. Let sit for 30 minutes then pass through a fine-meshed sieve to extract the flowers and leaves.

Heat a large saucepan over medium-high heat and add 1 tablespoon of the olive oil. When the oil is hot, add the carrot and onion and cook, stirring often, for 10 minutes, or until the carrot just starts to take on some color. Drain the soaked beans and add to the pan along with the stock, garlic, and cherries. Bring to a boil. Decrease the heat to achieve a simmer and cook, uncovered, until the beans are very tender, about 30 minutes. Add more stock if necessary during cooking to keep the beans covered. Keep warm.

Preheat the oven to 450°F. Season the lamb with the seasoned salt. (Reserve any leftover salt for another purpose.) Heat an ovenproof sauté pan over high heat and add the remaining 1 tablespoon olive oil. When the oil is hot, add the lamb and sear until golden brown on the underside, about 2 minutes. Turn the lamb over and place the pan in the oven. Roast for about 12 minutes for medium rare, until the internal temperature registers 120°F on an instant-read thermometer. Remove from the oven, loosely cover with aluminum foil, and let rest for 5 minutes.

Add the chard to the beans and cook over medium heat for about 2 minutes, until the chard is wilted and the beans are hot.

To serve, divide the beans and chard among 4 plates and top each serving with a lamb chop. Garnish with the parsley and serve immediately.

Roasted Rack of Lamb with Pomegranate Sauce

A rack of lamb is an elegant cut of meat and one of the easiest to roast; it is the whole rib section on one side of the animal, consisting of seven to eight chops. Because there can be a significant size variation between domestic and Australian or New Zealand lamb (see Kimball's headnote on page 85), I use the rule of thumb of a half pound of lamb per person—two to three chops. Be sure to adjust your cooking times accordingly if you do use the larger domestic rack, as I used the smaller New Zealand racks in this dish. To save time, have your butcher neatly trim each rack. If you have chops left over, they make great cold sandwiches the following day.

To juice a pomegranate, remove the seeds from the skin and membrane, put them in a strainer over a small bowl, and mash them with the back of a wooden spoon. For the 6 tablespoons called for in this recipe, you'd need two pomegranates. You can also buy the juice unsweetened in bottles or as a syrup or concentrate. Try health food stores or Middle Eastern markets if you can't find it in your grocery. I like to prepare basmati rice flavored with cinnamon as a side dish with this rack. Uncork a bottle of Cabernet Sauvignon, one that is full bodied and rich with the fruit flavors of cherries and currants, or try a Syrah that is jammy in character, which complements the sauce. GW

2 cloves garlic, pressed

½ teaspoon kosher salt

½ teaspoon freshly ground black pepper

1 tablespoon freshly squeezed lemon juice

2 racks of lamb (about 1½ pounds total) fully trimmed

Sauce

6 tablespoons pomegranate juice

1 tablespoon soy sauce

2 tablespoons rice vinegar

2½ teaspoons sesame oil

2 tablespoons freshly squeezed lemon juice

2 tablespoons sugar

Preheat the oven to 400°F with the rack in the upper middle position.

In a small bowl, combine the garlic, salt, pepper, and lemon juice and mix well. Place the racks, rib sides down, in a baking dish and spread the garlic mixture over the tops and sides. To prevent the ribs from burning, cover the tips with aluminum foil. Place the dish in the oven and roast for about 30 minutes for medium-rare, until the internal temperature registers 125°F on an instant-read thermometer. The meat should be rosy pink and lightly springy when pressed. Remove from the oven, loosely cover with foil, and let rest for 10 minutes before slicing.

To prepare the sauce, in a small saucepan over high heat, combine the pomegranate juice, soy sauce, rice vinegar, sesame oil, lemon juice, and sugar. Bring to a boil, then decrease the heat and simmer for about 20 minutes, until reduced to about ¼ cup.

To serve, cut each rack in half and divide among 4 plates, with 2 to 3 chops per person. Spoon the sauce over the meat and serve immediately.

Desserts

The gamut of desserts offered runs from cheeses and fruit to pure decadence. Look here if you would like . . .

Something sweet!

A pleasant finish to a delicious repast

A complement to a favorite dessert wine

Something to serve at a special occasion

Treats for a Sunday brunch

Blood Orange Sorbet with Orange Pastry Sticks

Sorbet

⅓ cup water

⅓ cup Sauterne-style dessert wine

1 cup sugar, more as needed

4 teaspoons finely grated blood orange zest

2½ cups freshly squeezed blood orange juice, strained

¼ recipe pastry sticks dough (page 113)

1 tablespoon finely grated orange zest

2 teaspoons plus 1 tablespoon sugar

¼ teaspoon ground ginger

Dessert wines made from Semillon and Sauvignon Blanc blends often have some citrus characteristics along with their sweet, rich flavors, making them a natural pairing for many fruit desserts. French Sauternes are the best known of these sweet wine blends. My family has been making a similar style of wine, which I like to use in this recipe, from our vineyards in California since the early 1930s. In our hillside orchard, there are several blood orange trees, which we begin harvesting in the winter months. The citrus from our trees can be tart, so I always taste the blood orange mixture prior to chilling the sorbet, and adjust the level of sweetness with more sugar if necessary. GW

To prepare the sorbet, in a small saucepan, combine the water, wine, sugar, and zest. Bring to a boil and remove from the heat. Stir in the blood orange juice. Taste for sweetness and adjust with sugar if necessary. Place the pan in a bowl of ice and stir until cool. Or, you can chill the mixture in the refrigerator.

Pour the cooled sorbet mixture into an ice cream maker and freeze according to the manufacturer's instructions.

Preheat the oven to 375°F. Butter a baking sheet.

To prepare the pastry sticks, follow the basic recipe, except separate the dough into 2 portions. Roll each portion into a rectangle ¹⁄₁₆ inch thick and brush the tops lightly with the beaten egg. Cut the rectangles in half crosswise with a fluted pastry cutter. In a small bowl, mix together the orange zest and 2 teaspoons sugar. Sprinkle the mixture over 2 pieces of the dough. Place the other 2 pieces, egg sides down, on top. Press the edges together to seal and gently roll once to press the sugar mixture into the dough. With the pastry cutter, cut the rectangles in half crosswise. Then cut lengthwise into ½-inch strips, about 6 inches long. Place the strips on the prepared baking sheet.

In a small bowl, mix together the 1 tablespoon sugar and the ginger. Sprinkle on the strips. Bake until light golden brown, about 15 minutes.

Scoop the sorbet into 4 dessert bowls. Place 1 to 2 pastry sticks to the side of each serving, and serve at once.

Apple-Almond Galette

This is a very easy dessert to put together at the last minute. You can use other fruits such as pears, peaches, or apricots instead of apples. This recipe works best with a tart apple, such as Granny Smith or Pippin. The finished galette has a consistency almost like that of a bar cookie. I especially enjoy drinking sweet, late harvest wines such as Sauternes, Alsatian Vendage Tardives, and Late Harvest Rieslings from Germany and America with this tart. *kg*

½ cup whole almonds, toasted (page 118)

4 ounces almond paste

¼ cup unsalted butter

¼ cup all-purpose flour

1 egg

1 tablespoon sugar

¼ teaspoon ground cinnamon

2 large apples, peeled, cored, and thinly sliced

1 recipe sweet pie dough, chilled (page 115)

Preheat the oven to 350°F. Line a baking sheet with parchment paper.

In a food processor, finely chop the almonds. Add the almond paste, butter, and flour and pulse until just mixed. Add the egg and process until it comes together into a dough-like consistency. (You could do all of this by hand.)

In a bowl, combine the sugar and cinnamon. Add the apples and toss well to coat. Taste and adjust the sugar if needed to retain a nice balance of acidity and sweetness—don't make them too sweet because the almond mixture has a lot of sweetness too.

Roll out the chilled dough into a round about 14 inches in diameter and ¼ inch thick. Trim the edges and place on the prepared baking sheet. Spread the almond mixture evenly on the dough, leaving a 2-inch uncovered border around the edges. Arrange the apples on top of the almond mixture in an overlapping circular pattern. Fold the border of the dough up over the filling toward the center, pleating every 3 to 4 inches to form a crust. Place in the oven and bake for about 1 hour, until golden brown. Cut into 12 slices and serve warm or at room temperature.

Meyer Lemon Soufflé

4 eggs, at room temperature, separated

¾ cup granulated sugar

Juice from 8 large Meyer lemons
(about ½ cup)

Finely grated zest of 1 lemon

1 tablespoon all-purpose flour

½ teaspoon pure almond extract

⅛ teaspoon salt

Confectioners' sugar, for dusting

Meyer lemons are becoming increasingly available in the produce sections of stores today. On our hillside, we have eight Meyer lemon trees, which are prolific throughout the year in our blessed California climate. A Meyer lemon is slightly sweeter and very juicy compared to other lemon varieties. If you cannot find Meyer lemons for this recipe, increase the sugar slightly to compensate for the more tart lemons or substitute 2 tablespoons of orange juice for lemon juice, which will add similar characteristics. If you like, you can butter and sugar the sides of your soufflé dish. I don't because I like the brown crust that forms.

Rather than using a soufflé dish, you can use about twelve lemon rinds to bake and serve the soufflé. Trim a flat end on each lemon so that it sits firmly. Cut about one-third of the lemon off the other end and set it aside for a garnish. Place a strainer over a small bowl and scoop out the pulp and juice into the strainer. Squeeze out the juice and use it in the recipe. Fill the lemons with the soufflé mixture up to the top edge and place the filled shells on a baking sheet lined with parchment paper. Bake in a 350F oven for about 15 minutes, until the tops are golden brown. Serve immediately, dusted with confectioners' sugar, and garnish the plates with the lemon tops. A late harvest Sauvignon Blanc–Semillon blend with rich honey-citrus flavors is one my favorite dessert wines with the soufflé. Gw

Preheat the oven to 350°F and place a rack in the center position. Bring several inches of water to a simmer in a pot large enough to hold a mixing bowl over, but not touching, the simmering water.

Place the egg yolks in the bowl of a stand mixer. Using the whisk attachment on medium speed, gradually beat ½ cup of the granulated sugar into the egg yolks and continue beating until the mixture turns pale yellow, about 5 minutes. With the motor running, add the lemon juice, zest, flour, and almond extract and continue to blend for another 2 minutes, until well blended. Set the bowl over the simmering water and whisk constantly until very thick, 10 to 12 minutes. Be careful not to overheat the mixture and scramble the egg yolks. Remove the bowl from the simmering water, return to the mixer, and beat on medium speed until cooled. Continually scrape down the sides to blend. Transfer to another bowl and set aside.

(continued)

Clean the mixer bowl thoroughly and add the egg whites and salt. Clean the whisk attachment and whisk the egg whites on low speed until soft peaks form. Sprinkle in the remaining $^1/_4$ cup granulated sugar, increase the speed to medium-high, and continue to beat until stiff, shiny peaks develop, about 5 minutes. Whisk one-third of the egg whites into the egg yolk mixture. Carefully fold in the remaining whites. Pour into a 2-quart soufflé dish or six 3-inch ramekins and place in the oven.

Bake the ramekins for 20 to 25 minutes or the large soufflé dish for 30 minutes, until lightly browned and a knife inserted into the center comes out clean. Dust with confectioners' sugar and serve immediately.

Apple Tart with
Late Harvest Riesling Ice Cream

Serves 4

All too often, desserts are sweeter than the wines they are served with, making the wine taste even less sweet. If the sweetness and acidity in a dessert are in balance, or neutralize each other, the wine will taste true and not be affected by the flavors in the dessert. The tartness in the apples and the light dusting of sugar on this tart help to balance its acidity and sweetness, making it a great partner for the Late Harvest Riesling. This recipe uses store-bought ice cream as a great shortcut to making your own wine-flavored ice cream. Of course, you could start from scratch, especially if you have an ice cream maker. *KJ*

1 pint store-bought vanilla ice cream

½ cup Late Harvest Riesling or other sweet or late harvest wine

1 (9 by 10-inch) sheet puff pastry dough, ¼ inch thick, thawed if frozen

4 Granny Smith or Gravenstein apples, peeled, cored, and thinly sliced

Sugar, for sprinkling

Ground cinnamon, for sprinkling

Place the ice cream in a bowl and leave at room temperature until it becomes soft enough to stir. Stir in the wine and place in the freezer to firm up. This may take anywhere from 20 minutes to 1 hour, depending on how soft the ice cream is. (The ice cream can be flavored a day in advance.)

Preheat the oven to 375°F.

Cut the sheet of dough into quarters, yielding 4 pieces about 4½ by 5 inches. On each piece, cut a strip of dough ½ inch wide from both sides of the 4½-inch length. Spread a light coating of water on the bottoms of the strips and place them on top of the dough, parallel with the edges they were cut from. This creates a little pastry trough with raised edges. (See illustration.) Arrange the apple slices between the edges in an overlapping pattern. Sprinkle with sugar and cinnamon.

Place in the oven and bake until golden brown, about 25 minutes. Every 10 minutes, rotate the pan from front to back to ensure even baking. Serve warm or at room temperature with a scoop of the ice cream on top, garnished with a sprinkle of cinnamon.

5"

4½"

Chocolate-Chile-Pecan Cake with Double Bourbon Whipped Cream

Makes one 10-inch cake; serves 12

1 Bourbon-Madagascar vanilla bean

¼ cup bourbon

¾ cup plus 2 tablespoons sugar

1½ cups pecans

½ pound bittersweet chocolate, grated, plus additional reserved for shaving

2 teaspoons pure vanilla extract

1 teaspoon medium-ground dried chiles (2 to 3 seeded chiles)

¼ teaspoon ground cinnamon

8 eggs, separated

½ teaspoon cream of tartar

1 cup heavy cream, well chilled

Chiles and chocolate? The combination has a history that dates back to pre-Columbian America. Some say the two together have a beguiling, aphrodisiac quality. For me, it may be the late harvest Zinfandels and ports I enjoy drinking with this moist, spicy cake. Be sure to use dried, ground chiles and not a commercial chili powder that usually contains additional ingredients such as garlic powder and dried herbs. You can use any kind of vanilla bean, but I like the Bourbon variety from Madagascar—it also makes a good recipe title! Using the grating attachment of your food processor will make grating the chocolate a snap. Remember to put the bowl and whisk for whipping the cream into the freezer 30 minutes before you are going to need them—the cream will whip faster. kj

Place a small saucepan over high heat. Cut the vanilla bean in half crosswise. Remove the saucepan from the heat and add the vanilla bean and bourbon. Place the pan back on the heat and carefully tip away from you so the flame ignites the alcohol. (If you have an electric stove, preheat the pan, add the vanilla bean and bourbon, and ignite with a match.) When the flames die down, remove the bean from the bourbon, split in half lengthwise, scrap out the seeds, and add to the bourbon. Discard the pod. Remove from the heat and allow to cool.

Preheat the oven to 350°F and place a rack in the center position. Butter a 10-inch springform pan. Line the bottom of the pan with parchment paper and butter the parchment paper. Sprinkle the bottom and sides with extra-fine sugar, shaking out any excess.

In a food processor, combine the ¾ cup sugar and the pecans and process until very fine. Transfer to a bowl and add the chocolate, vanilla, chile, cinnamon, and egg yolks. Stir until well blended.

Place the egg whites in another bowl, sprinkle with the cream of tartar, and whip with an electric mixer on medium speed until stiff peaks form. One-third at a time, fold the whites into the chocolate mixture. Pour the batter into the prepared pan and place in the oven. Cook for about 30 minutes, until the center of the cake is just set. Shake the pan lightly. If it doesn't jiggle, it's done. Remove from the oven and place on a wire rack. While the cake is still hot, run a very thin-bladed knife around the edge of the pan to loosen it. Remove the outer ring of the pan and allow the cake to cool completely.

In a chilled bowl, combine the cooled bourbon mixture, the 2 table-spoons sugar, and the cream and whip with an electric mixer on medium speed until soft peaks form. Slice the cake and divide among dessert plates. Scoop a dollop of the bourbon cream on each slice of cake. Garnish with shaved chocolate and serve immediately.

Mango Ice Cream

Makes 1½ quarts; serves 12

This is a great way to use fruit that has become a little overripe. Peaches, nectarines, and strawberries work well too. The small amount of citrus juice, in this case lime juice, helps to balance the sweetness of the mango. This ice cream goes well with sweet, late harvest white wines. KJ

3 (12-ounce) very ripe mangoes

1 tablespoon freshly squeezed lime juice

1½ cups milk

6 egg yolks

¾ cup sugar

1½ cups heavy cream

Peel the mangoes and slice the flesh from the pit, squeezing as much juice as you can from the pit into a small bowl. Purée the flesh, juice, and lime juice in a blender or food processor.

Bring the milk to a boil in a nonreactive saucepan over medium-high heat. Remove the pan from the heat. In a bowl, whisk together the yolks and sugar until pale in color. Add the hot milk, a little at a time, whisking with each addition. Thoroughly blend each addition before adding more, to bring the temperature of the egg yolks up to the temperature of the cream without scrambling the yolks. Return the mixture to the saucepan and cook over medium heat until thickened, 5 to 7 minutes. Do not let it boil. The mixture should coat the back of a spoon and hold a line when you draw your finger through it. Pass through a fine-meshed sieve into a bowl set inside a larger bowl filled with ice. Whisk in the mango purée and cream. Stir until cool.

Freeze in an ice cream maker according to the manufacturer's instructions. Scoop into bowls to serve.

Peach-Berry Cobbler with Meyer Lemon Crust

Serves 6

My grandmother taught me this recipe. We would make it together when there was an abundance of Babcock or white peaches in her orchard and black-berries along the creekside. At my house today, we have numerous Meyer lemon trees that provide citrus nearly year-round. I have incorporated the Meyer lemon into Grandmother's crust, which is almost cookie-like when baked. If you don't have Meyer lemons, Eureka or other lemon varieties can be substituted. A scoop of vanilla ice cream or Kimball's Late Harvest Riesling ice cream (page 97) is superb with the cobbler. I also enjoy serving this dish with a glass of port or Late Harvest Riesling. GW

Preheat the oven to 375°F and place a rack in the center position. Butter a shallow 2-quart casserole.

To make the filling, combine the peaches, blackberries, sugar, and cornstarch in a bowl and set aside for 5 to 10 minutes. Stir a couple of times to make sure the sugar dissolves.

To make the crust, combine the flour, baking powder, and salt in a small bowl. In a stand mixer or food processor, cream together the butter and sugar until smooth. Beat in the egg, lemon juice, lemon zest, and vanilla. Slowly add the flour mixture and blend until the dough becomes consistently moist throughout, about 2 minutes.

Pour the fruit into the casserole and spoon dollops of the crust on top, spacing the dough evenly as it will spread as it bakes. Bake for about 45 minutes, until the juices are bubbling, the crust is golden brown, and the fruit is tender when pierced with a fork. Allow to cool slightly. Divide among 6 bowls and serve.

Filling
5 to 6 firm, ripe peaches, peeled, pitted and cut into ¾-inch wedges (5 to 6 cups)

3 cups blackberries

½ cup sugar

1 tablespoon cornstarch

Crust
½ cup plus 2 tablespoons all-purpose flour

¼ teaspoon baking powder

¼ teaspoon salt

½ cup unsalted butter, at room temperature

½ cup sugar

1 egg, beaten

1 tablespoon freshly squeezed Meyer lemon juice

2 teaspoons grated Meyer lemon zest

½ teaspoon pure vanilla extract

Sour Cream Sorbet with Strawberry Soup

Sorbet

2 cups water

¾ cup granulated sugar

2 cups sour cream (low-fat is okay)

1 teaspoon finely minced lemon zest

½ teaspoon freshly squeezed
   lemon juice

2 pints fresh strawberries

2 tablespoons balsamic vinegar

2 tablespoons confectioners' sugar,
   plus more as needed

I first made this recipe while vacationing with friends in the Chianti Classico region of Italy. I wanted to make a simple dessert that would take advantage of the incredible in-season strawberries. I used whole-milk yogurt the first time I made it, but it works just as well with sour cream, as I've done here. That first time, I didn't have an ice cream machine so I made it as a granita. To do this, place the combined liquids in a shallow pan in the freezer. For several hours, stir every 10 to 15 minutes with a couple of forks. Keep doing this until it is completely frozen. The final consistency is like little crystals of ice. We drank a wonderful Vin Santo with it that night. KJ

To prepare the sorbet, combine the water and granulated sugar in a saucepan over high heat. Bring to a boil, then remove from the heat and allow to cool.

In a bowl, combine the sour cream, zest, and lemon juice. Whisk in the sugar water. Pour into an ice cream maker and freeze according to the manufacturer's instructions. (Mine takes about 20 minutes.)

Hull the strawberries and cut lengthwise into quarters. In a bowl, combine half of the strawberries with the balsamic vinegar and confectioners' sugar. You may need to add more sugar depending on the sweetness of the berries. Let the sweetened berries sit for 15 minutes. Transfer to a food processor and purée until smooth, then pass through a medium-meshed sieve into a bowl. Discard the seeds. Combine the purée with the remaining strawberries. Taste and adjust the sweetness with sugar if necessary.

To serve, ladle the strawberry soup into bowls, and top each with a scoop of sorbet.

Butternut Squash Brownie

This great fall recipe from our pastry chef at the restaurant, Michelle Lyon, is wonderful on its own, but even better when served with ice cream and chocolate and caramel sauces as a sundae. You can follow the instructions below to make the butternut squash purée or you can substitute 1 1/2 cups canned pumpkin. I prefer the flavor of a fresh winter squash, which gives a subtle undercurrent of fall flavor to the brownies, as well as adding extra moisture. Port, late harvest Muscat, or Hungarian Tokay are especially good with this brownie. KJ

1/2 butternut squash, seeded

5 ounces unsweetened chocolate

1/2 cup plus 3 tablespoons unsalted butter

4 large eggs

1/2 teaspoon kosher salt

2 cups sugar

1 1/2 teaspoons pure vanilla extract

1 1/4 cups plus 2 tablespoons all-purpose flour

3/4 teaspoon baking powder

Preheat the oven to 375°F.

Place the squash in a baking dish, cut side up. Add 1/2 inch of water and cover the dish with aluminum foil. Roast for 1 1/4 to 1 1/2 hours, until very tender. Scoop out the flesh and purée in a blender or food processor. Measure out 1 1/2 cups of the purée for this recipe. (The squash can be cooked in advance.)

Decrease the oven temperature to 350°F. Line the bottom of a 9 by 13-inch baking dish with parchment paper.

Bring several inches of water to a simmer in a pan large enough to hold a smaller saucepan over, but not touching, the simmering water. Add the chocolate and butter to the smaller saucepan and melt together, stirring frequently. When the mixture is melted and blended together, about 5 minutes, remove from the heat and set aside to cool.

Using an electric mixer on low speed or by hand, whip together the eggs, salt, sugar, and vanilla in a bowl until thick and pale yellow. Fold the chocolate mixture into the egg mixture and then fold in the squash. In a bowl, combine the flour and baking powder, then fold into the wet ingredients. Pour into the prepared baking dish and smooth over the top. Bake for 20 to 25 minutes, until the middle springs back when lightly pressed. Remove from the oven and place on a wire rack to cool.

When cool, loosen the edges of the brownie from the pan with a knife. Turn over onto a baking sheet and remove the parchment paper. Turn back into the baking dish and cut into squares. Serve immediately.

Ginger Poached Pear Tart

1 (750-ml) bottle sweet wine such as Riesling, Sauterne, or Muscat de Beaume-de-Venise

3¼ cups water

Zest of 1 orange, cut into strips

Juice of 1 orange

Zest of 1 lemon, cut into strips

Juice of 1 lemon

Zest of 1 lime, cut into strips

Juice of 1 lime

¼ cup sliced peeled fresh ginger (about a 4-inch piece)

2 cinnamon sticks

12 whole cloves

½ cup sugar

4 Bosc or Anjou pears, peeled, halved, and cored

1 recipe chilled pastry cream, prepared with 1 teaspoon finely grated lemon zest stirred in before cooling (page 112)

1 (12-inch tart pan) sweet pie dough crust, fully cooked and cooled (page 115)

I created this ginger-infused pear-poaching liquid for a trip to Hong Kong, where I prepared a dinner to showcase Wente Vineyards' wines. I wanted to make a dessert that used Western cooking techniques but would be at home in either the East or the West. I looked to Asian ingredients as the bridge. Citrus fruits and ginger, both natives of eastern Asia, have been part of Western cooking for centuries, yet still evoke their origins; pears originated in the Caucasus Mountains of Asia and spread both east and west. The ginger and citrus in the poaching liquid enhance and complement each other, accentuating the milder flavors in the pears. The flavorings in this tart can easily be varied. Try seasoning the pears with other ingredients such as cinnamon or star anise or add chocolate, vanilla, or almond extract to the pastry cream. If you are having a dinner party and want to get ahead of the game, you can prepare the poached pears, pastry cream, and sweet pie dough a day in advance. However, it is best to bake the shell and fill it right before guests arrive to prevent it from getting soggy. I like to serve the same wine I used in the poaching liquid along with the dessert, so when you buy your wine, buy two bottles—one to cook with, one to serve. KJ

Combine the wine, water, citrus zests and juices, ginger, cinnamon, cloves, and sugar in a nonreactive saucepan over high heat. Add the pears and bring to a boil. Remove from the heat and set the pan aside to cool; the pears will cook as the liquid cools.

To assemble the tart, spoon the pastry cream into the tart shell and spread evenly. Remove the pears from the poaching liquid and cut crosswise into ¼-inch slices. Starting from the outside edge of the tart shell, overlap the pear slices in concentric circles on top of the pastry cream. It will look somewhat like a rose. Slice and serve immediately.

Gorgonzola and Fig Tart

18 fresh Mission figs

1 teaspoon dry red wine

2 teaspoons pure maple syrup

4 (5 by 5-inch) pieces puff pastry, thawed if frozen

¼ cup Gorgonzola cheese

1 tablespoon slivered almonds

I tried Stilton and Roquefort cheeses before deciding on the Gorgonzola for this tart. The creaminess of Gorgonzola is a perfect foil for figs, which can best be found fresh from late summer through fall. This is a subtly sweet tart that is wonderful for a nice leisurely dessert enjoyed with a good bottle of vintage port. KG

Preheat the oven to 375°F. Line a baking sheet with parchment paper.

Trim the stem ends off the figs and cut in half lengthwise. In a bowl, combine the wine and maple syrup and mix well. Add the figs and toss well to coat.

Place the puff pastry squares on the prepared baking sheet. Put 1 table-spoon of Gorgonzola in the middle of each square and spread it out to within 1 inch of all edges. On each square, arrange 9 fig halves, cut sides up, on top of the cheese in 3 rows, leaving the outer edges of the puff pastry uncovered. Drizzle any remaining wine syrup over the figs, dividing it equally among the tarts. Sprinkle the almonds evenly over the tarts.

Place in the oven and bake until the bottom and edges of the pastry are golden brown, about 15 minutes. Serve immediately.

Chocolate Chunk and Pecan Cookies

If you love cakey cookies, these are for you! The big chunks of chocolate give the baked cookies a pleasantly unique texture. Make the chocolate chunks by coarsely chopping a piece of block chocolate into pecan-sized pieces. Once you have formed the dough into balls, you can bake them right away, freeze them, or refrigerate for a few hours until you are ready to eat them (they don't stay around once they are out of the oven!). Yummy with port or Late Harvest Zinfandel. KJ

Preheat the oven to 350°F.

Using the paddle attachment in a stand mixer, cream together the butter, brown sugar, and granulated sugar until light and fluffy. Add the eggs, one at a time, blending in each egg before adding the next. Add the salt and vanilla and mix until combined.

In a bowl, combine the flour, baking soda, and pecans. Add to the butter mixture and blend well. Remove the bowl from the mixer and fold in the chocolate chips and chunks. Using about ¼ cup dough per cookie, form the dough into balls. Place on a baking sheet about 3 inches apart and bake until light golden brown, 8 to 10 minutes. Transfer to wire racks to cool. Serve immediately or store for up to 1 week in an airtight container.

1 cup unsalted butter, at room temperature

1½ cups firmly packed dark brown sugar

½ cup granulated sugar

2 eggs

1 teaspoon kosher salt

1 tablespoon pure vanilla extract

2¾ cups all-purpose flour

1 tablespoon baking soda

1½ cups whole pecans, hand crumbled

1 cup semisweet chocolate chips

1 cup bittersweet chocolate chunks

Basics

We've included some basic recipes and methods to make meal preparation easier. Here you'll find . . .

Some dough recipes

A few preparations for use in desserts

Some stocks

A starting place for making aioli

A few basic techniques

Aioli

1 teaspoon chopped garlic

1 extra large egg yolk

2 tablespoons freshly squeezed lemon juice

1 teaspoon Dijon mustard

1 cup olive oil

Kosher salt and freshly ground black pepper

If one were making aioli in the traditional manner, the whole process would take place in a mortar and pestle. This is the gentlest way to incorporate the olive oil without making it bitter—olive oil is a very delicate creature and doesn't like to be overworked. For food safety reasons, we do add a bit of heat to the preparation. I usually begin the process in a mortar and pestle and then transfer to a bowl to finish it up. *kj*

In a mortar and pestle, crush the garlic until it forms a smooth paste. Add the egg yolk and lemon juice and combine until smooth. Transfer to a nonreactive heatproof bowl, place over a pan of barely simmering water (not too hot or the egg yolk will scramble), and whisk constantly until the mixture starts to thicken, 4 to 5 minutes. Remove from the heat and whisk in the mustard. Whisk in the olive oil, a few drops at a time at first, and then in a slow, steady stream until all is added. Season with salt and pepper. Refrigerate until needed. Aioli will keep in the refrigerator for 1 to 2 days, but you should use it as quickly as possible as the flavor will change with time.

1 teaspoon chopped garlic

1 cup store-bought mayonnaise

1 teaspoon freshly squeezed lemon juice

¼ cup extra virgin olive oil

If you don't have the time to start from scratch, try this shortcut:
In a mortar and pestle, crush the garlic until it forms a smooth paste. In a small bowl, combine the mayonnaise and the lemon juice. Whisk in the olive oil. Add the garlic paste and mix until well blended.

Bread Crumbs

Bread crumbs are a wonderful way to use up leftover, stale bread that would otherwise go to waste. Our recipes call for two types—fresh and toasted. Initially, they are prepared the same way: Cut the bread into bite-sized pieces. If you leave the crust on you will get a deeper flavor. Place in a food processor and process until fine. I like to put the crumbs through a large-meshed sieve and then process the larger pieces again. If you want really fine crumbs, you can put them through a finer screen.

For toasted bread crumbs, preheat the oven to 350°F. Thinly spread the fresh bread crumbs on a baking sheet. Toast until light golden brown, 15 to 20 minutes. Halfway through toasting, stir with a spatula to encourage even browning. Bread crumbs will keep for up to 1 week at room temperature in resealable plastic bags, or freeze for longer storage. *kj*

Chicken Stock

Of all the stocks, chicken is the one I use the most since its flavor is more neutral than other stocks, such as fish or veal. I always buy a whole chicken whenever I am cooking chicken for dinner. I cut it into pieces, saving the backs and necks in the freezer for making stock. When I have enough chicken saved up, I fill my five-gallon stockpot and make stock. It's easy to double the recipe and then freeze the stock in quart-sized freezer bags for future use. KJ

Place the chicken bones and water in a large nonreactive stockpot and bring to a boil over high heat. Decrease the heat to achieve a simmer and stir to bring most of the impurities and fat to the surface. Thoroughly skim the surface. Add enough water to bring the stock back to the original level. Increase the heat to high. Add the leek, onion, celery, carrot, garlic, wine, parsley stems, thyme, peppercorns, and bay leaves and bring to a boil. Decrease the heat to achieve a simmer and cook for 6 to 8 hours, skimming once an hour. Do not cook at too high a temperature or the stock will be cloudy. Remove from the heat and pass through a medium-meshed sieve. Chicken stock will keep for 1 week in the refrigerator and up to several months in the freezer.

5 pounds chicken bones, preferably backs and necks

4 quarts water, more as needed

½ cup thinly sliced leek, including white and green parts

½ cup sliced yellow onion

¼ cup chopped celery

¾ cup chopped carrot

1 whole head garlic, halved

1 cup dry white wine

Stems from ¼ bunch flat-leaf parsley (leaves removed)

¼ bunch thyme

1½ teaspoons black peppercorns

2 bay leaves

Cornmeal Tart Dough

The inclusion of olive oil and cornmeal in this dough creates a moist and pleasing texture, making the dough work well in more rustic recipes such as savory galettes and tarts. Be careful not to add too much water as it will overwork the dough, making it tough. Treat it gently! GW

In a bowl, combine the flour, cornmeal, sugar, and salt. Using a pastry blender, work in the butter until the dough resembles coarse bread crumbs. A few pea-sized pieces are okay. In a small bowl, whisk together the olive oil and water and, still using the pastry blender, gradually add to the dough mixture until the dough starts to come together. Depending on your flour and the humidity, you may not need all the oil-water mixture, or you may need a little more water to make the dough come together.

With your hands, gently work the dough against the bowl, until it holds together and isn't sticky. Shape the dough into a flat disk about 4 inches across. Wrap in plastic and refrigerate for 1 hour before rolling out.

1 cup all-purpose flour

⅓ cup coarse yellow cornmeal

1 teaspoon sugar

1 teaspoon salt

6 tablespoons cold unsalted butter, cut into ½-inch pieces

3 tablespoons olive oil

5 to 6 tablespoons ice water, as needed

Crème Fraîche

3/4 cup plus 2 tablespoons heavy cream
  (7 parts)

2 tablespoons cultured buttermilk
  (1 part)

This version of soured cream is very easy to make at home and has a much better flavor than commercial sour cream. It has the added benefit of not separating when you cook with it. Use an active cultured buttermilk, since the lactic acid bacteria it contains is needed to sour the cream. *Kj*

In a saucepan, over low heat, warm the cream to body temperature, about 3 minutes. If too hot, the culture will die and the crème won't thicken. Whisk in the buttermilk and transfer to a bowl or jar. Cover tightly and put in a warm place until thickened, 8 to 24 hours. After thickening, it will keep for up to 10 days in the refrigerator.

Makes about 3 cups

Pastry Cream

2 cups milk

1/2 cup sugar

2 tablespoons plus 2 teaspoons
  cornstarch

2 large eggs

1/4 cup unsalted butter, melted

Pastry cream provides a rich, custardy texture with enough body to hold together many desserts; it functions both as a binder and a filling. Pastry cream can be flavored by adding ingredients directly to it or by steeping items such as nuts, coffee beans, vanilla beans, or herbs in the milk-sugar mixture. To do this, bring the milk and sugar to a boil with the flavoring agent and let it sit until the flavor comes through, usually 1 to 2 hours. Strain the liquid and proceed with the recipe. *Kj*

In a heavy-bottomed saucepan, combine 1 1/2 cups of the milk and the sugar and bring to a boil over high heat. In a bowl, whisk together the remaining 1/2 cup milk and the cornstarch, making sure there are no lumps. Whisk the eggs into the cornstarch mixture. Add this mixture to the boiling milk and sugar and whisk continuously until it returns to a boil. Remove from the heat and stir in the melted butter.

Pour into a shallow, nonreactive baking dish with a large surface area. Cover with plastic wrap, placing it directly on the surface to prevent a skin from forming. Cool in the freezer for about 10 minutes, then move to the refrigerator if you are not going to use right away. It will keep for 1 day.

Pastry Sticks

There are many variations for this dough. You can create savory toppings or fillings by combining different herbs and cheeses. You can also sprinkle the dough with combinations of sugar and citrus zests to make dessert accompaniments. Some of my savory favorites include goat cheese and basil, cumin and cayenne, or simply herbes de Provence. Favorite sweet blends include cinnamon and finely ground nuts, or chopped toasted almonds and grated lemon zest pressed into the dough. You could also use a savory mixture on half of the dough and a sweet topping on the remainder. I use the egg wash in different ways—sometimes to help adhere the topping to the dough, sometimes as a wash. You can make the sticks up to 3 or 4 days ahead of time and keep them in an airtight container. Or, freeze them and remove them from the freezer a couple of hours before serving. To serve warm, heat in a low-temperature oven. GW

1½ cups all-purpose flour

½ teaspoon kosher salt

½ cup cold unsalted butter, cut into ¼-inch pieces

3 tablespoons freshly squeezed lemon juice

1 large egg, beaten

Preheat the oven to 375°F. Butter a baking sheet.

Using the pastry blade in a food processor, combine the flour and salt. Add the butter and pulse until the mixture forms ¼-inch crumbs. Gradually add the lemon juice and pulse until moistened. (To do this by hand, combine the flour and salt in a bowl, add the butter, and use a pastry blender to work the mixture into ¼-inch crumbs. Then mix in the lemon juice.) The dough should hold together but not be sticky when you gently squeeze a small handful into a ball. If it doesn't, sprinkle in more lemon juice.

On a lightly floured surface, press the dough into a ½-inch-thick rectangle. Lightly flour a rolling pin and roll the dough from the center outward to about ⅛ inch thick. Using a fluted pastry wheel, trim the dough to a 12 by 15-inch rectangle. Cut into quarters. Cut each piece lengthwise into strips about ½ inch wide by 6 inches long. Brush with the egg and transfer to the prepared baking sheet.

Bake until light golden brown, about 15 minutes. If your oven is big enough, you can cook 2 sheets at a time, but watch them to make sure they brown evenly. You may have to switch the baking sheets around to make sure one sheet doesn't brown quicker. Let the sticks cool on the sheets for a couple of minutes, then transfer to a wire rack to cool completely.

Pizza Dough

2 cups warm water

1 tablespoon plus 1 teaspoon
active dry yeast

1 tablespoon sugar

1 tablespoon kosher salt

6 tablespoons olive oil

4¼ cups bread flour, more as needed

This pizza dough is designed to rise fairly quickly, with a strong, stretchy structure. The sugar and warm water added at the beginning activate the yeast. If the water is too hot, the yeast cells will be killed. Salt inhibits the growth of yeast, so it is added with the rest of the ingredients, after the yeast has been activated. You can make this dough using less yeast, but it will take longer to rise.

Thorough kneading of the dough activates and strengthens the gluten in the flour, giving it the structure that allows the dough to stretch nicely without breaking. I use bread flour in this recipe because it has a higher gluten content, which makes a stronger dough. Letting the dough rest and rise gently lightens it, which also helps in the shaping process. You may need to use more or less flour than called for in the recipe. The capacity of the flour to retain water changes depending on the weather and humidity, and from one wheat harvest to another. Many chefs don't measure, preferring to determine the right amount by eye and feel. The dough freezes well, so make the whole amount and use portions as you need them.   *KJ*

To prepare in a stand mixer, combine the water, yeast, and sugar in the bowl of the mixer. Let rest for about 10 minutes, until the sugar dissolves and the yeast starts to bloom, forming a foamy surface on the water. With the dough hook, mix in the salt and olive oil on low speed. Slowly add the flour until the dough starts to pull away from the sides of the bowl. The dough should be fairly wet and sticky to the touch. Knead with the dough hook at high speed for 3 to 4 minutes, then decrease the speed to medium and knead for 5 minutes. Turn out onto a floured work surface and knead by hand for 3 to 4 minutes, until smooth.

To prepare by hand, combine the water, yeast, and sugar in a large bowl. Let sit for 10 minutes, until the sugar dissolves and the yeast starts to bloom. Add the salt and olive oil and stir well. Slowly stir in the flour with a wooden spoon. Add just enough to be able to work the dough; it should still be a little sticky. Transfer to a floured surface and knead by hand for 15 minutes, until smooth.

Oil the sides of a bowl that is at least twice the size of the dough, place the dough in the bowl, and cover with a towel. Let rise in a warm place for about 1 hour, until doubled in volume.

Remove the dough from the bowl and punch down to release any air bubbles. Divide into 8 equal portions for pizzettas or 4 portions for pizza. On a lightly floured surface, roll each portion into a tight ball. Place on a lightly floured baking sheet and cover with plastic wrap. Let rest in the refrigerator for 30 minutes before using. The dough can rest in the refrigerator for 3 to 4 hours, or it can be frozen for longer storage. If you freeze the dough, let it defrost in the refrigerator for at least 3 to 4 hours before using.

To shape the dough, dust your hands with flour and begin slowly stretching the dough, always working from the outside edge. Stretch and shape the dough into rounds. If you don't feel comfortable with this method, on a lightly floured surface, use a rolling pin to roll the dough out into the size for your pizzettas or pizzas. Place the dough on a floured pizza paddle or on the back of a floured baking sheet. Arrange the toppings on the dough and cook according to the recipe instructions.

Sweet Pie Dough

Makes two 9-inch pie shells or one 12-inch tart shell (with a little left over)

The sugar in this recipe makes the dough much more forgiving when it's rolled out. Although not as flaky as unsweetened pie dough, it is very tender and holds together well in both small and large tarts. The dough can also be hand-pressed into tart pans or shells, making it much easier to line smaller baking pans. Wrapped securely in plastic wrap, it will keep for 4 to 5 days in the refrigerator or 1 month in the freezer. KJ

5 cups all-purpose flour

3/4 cup sugar

1 tablespoon kosher salt

1 1/2 cups cold unsalted butter, cut into small pieces

1/3 cup egg yolks (about 5 large egg yolks)

1/4 cup cold water, more as needed

To prepare in a stand mixer, using the paddle attachment on low speed, combine the flour, sugar, and salt. Add the butter in small pieces and mix for about 2 1/2 minutes, until the mixture resembles coarse cornmeal. Remove the bowl from the mixer. Using your hands, check to see that there are not too many big lumps of butter. A few actually help to make the pastry more flaky. Return the bowl to the mixer and add the egg yolks and water. Mix on low speed until the dough just begins to hold together, about 2 minutes. You may need to add more cold water if it is too dry. Remove the dough from the mixer, wrap in plastic wrap, and flatten slightly with your hands. Refrigerate for 30 minutes.

To prepare by hand, combine the flour, sugar, and salt in a bowl. Cut the butter into the dry ingredients with a pastry cutter, a fork, or your hands. Blend until it resembles coarse cornmeal. Add the egg yolks and water and mix until the dough just holds together. You may need to add more cold water if it is too dry. Remove the dough from the bowl, wrap in plastic wrap, and flatten slightly with your hands. Refrigerate for 30 minutes.

(continued)

To roll out, lightly dust a work surface and the top of the dough with flour. Working from the center with a rolling pin, roll the dough into a circle about ¼ inch thick. Roll the dough onto the rolling pin, and then roll it off into the tart or pie pan, centering the dough in the pan. Press the dough into the bottom and sides of the pan. With a sharp knife, trim the excess dough from the top. Use the trimmings to patch any holes. Place the shell in the refrigerator for 30 minutes.

To bake an unfilled pie or tart shell, preheat the oven to 350°F. Press a piece of aluminum foil into the shell and place an empty pie tin on top of the foil. This will help prevent shrinkage during cooking. Another method is to line the shell with parchment paper or foil and fill it with beans or pie weights.

For a partially baked shell, bake until the middle of the shell has lost its rawness, 10 to 15 minutes. A partially cooked shell will have an even blond color throughout.

For a fully cooked shell, remove the extra tin and aluminum foil (or beans) after 10 to 15 minutes, return to the oven, and cook until golden brown throughout, about 15 minutes.

Veal Stock

Makes about 4 quarts

4 pounds veal bones, preferably shanks and marrow bones

½ cup thinly sliced leek, white part only

½ cup sliced yellow onion

¼ cup chopped celery

¾ cup chopped carrot

2 tablespoons olive oil

1 cup dry red wine

4 quarts water, more as needed

1 whole head garlic, halved

1 cup canned peeled tomatoes, with juice

Stems from ¼ bunch flat-leaf parsley

¼ bunch fresh thyme

1½ teaspoons black peppercorns

2 bay leaves

When making veal stock, try to use marrow bones since the natural gelatin in the marrow will thicken the stock. To remove the most fat during skimming, use a ladle and concentrate on the outside edge of the pot, away from where it bubbles—this is where the fat accumulates. Always start stocks with cold water, which allows the meat to release its impurities (soluble proteins) slowly, so they rise to the top and are easily skimmed. As with all stocks, this recipe is easily doubled, and any extra can be frozen for longer storage. KJ

Preheat the oven to 350°F. In a heavy roasting pan, combine the veal bones, leek, onion, celery, and carrot. Toss with the olive oil and place in the oven. Roast, turning every 15 minutes, for 40 to 50 minutes, until golden brown. Transfer the bones and vegetables to a large stockpot. Drain off any excess oil or fat left in the roasting pan and place over medium heat. Add the wine to the pan and stir to scrape up the browned bits from the bottom of the pan. Add to the stockpot along with the water, garlic, tomatoes, parsley stems, thyme, peppercorns, and bay leaves.

Place the pot over high heat and bring to a boil. Decrease the heat to achieve a simmer and stir to bring most of the impurities and fat to the surface. Thoroughly skim the surface. Add enough water to bring the stock back to the original level. Increase the heat to high and bring to a boil. Decrease the heat to achieve a simmer and cook for 12 to 24 hours, skimming occasionally as fat rises to the top and adding water as needed to keep the stock at the same level. The longer you let the stock simmer, the better the flavors will be. Do not cook at too high a temperature or the stock will be cloudy. Remove from the heat and pass through a medium-meshed sieve. Veal stock will keep for 1 week in the refrigerator and up to several months in the freezer.

Veal Demi-Glace

Makes about 2 quarts

A demi-glace is stock reduced by half for more intense flavor. Make the veal stock as described above. After the stock has been strained, place it in a pot over low heat and simmer slowly until reduced by half, about 1 hour. The lower the heat during reduction, the better the flavor.

Pizza Oven Preparation

To prevent it from cracking, a pizza stone needs to start heating in a cold oven and cool along with the oven after it is used. Place a pizza stone on the bottom of the oven or on the bottom rack. (If you do not have a pizza stone, cover the bottom of the oven or the bottom rack with bricks.) Turn the temperature to the highest baking setting possible, usually 500°F. The oven will take a bit longer to reach the required temperature with the addition of the stone or bricks.

When the pizza is ready, slide it onto the stone or bricks to bake, keeping the oven temperature at 500°F. If you do not have a stone or bricks for your oven, simply place the pizza on a baking sheet and bake on the lowest rack. It may take a few minutes longer to cook.

Toasting Nuts

Toasting enhances the flavor of many nuts. Preheat the oven to 350°F. Spread the nuts on an ungreased baking sheet. Bake for 4 to 8 minutes for small nuts, such as pine nuts or sliced almonds, and 8 to 10 minutes for large nuts, such as pecans and walnuts (the time will vary depending on the kind of nuts you are toasting). The nuts should be lightly toasted and crisp but not browned. Stir or shake the pan very frequently to avoid burning, about every 3 minutes. All nuts burn quickly, so watch very carefully.

To remove the skins from toasted nuts, such as hazelnuts, rub them between your palms, between two sheets of waxed paper, or in a clean kitchen towel after they have cooled. Be sure to store nuts in airtight containers, as their oils can turn rancid. Stored properly, toasted nuts will keep for up to 4 months at room temperature or 6 months in the freezer.

Water Baths

Water baths are used when it is important to keep an overall, even heat during baking. The hardest part of the whole process is getting the water bath into the oven without spilling it. To accomplish this, bring a teakettleful of water to a boil. Place your prepared dish into a larger pan for the water bath, and place both pans in the oven. Then pour the boiling water into the larger pan to come halfway up the sides of the smaller dish. This also helps with cooking times, as you are not waiting for the water to reach oven temperature.

Index

THE CASUAL VINEYARD TABLE